Magnify the Lord

A Challenge to the Nominal Christian

Matt Drayer

Sermon on the Mount Publishing
Manchester, MI

Copyright © 2014 Matthew Drayer. The material in this book may be used noncommercially for the advancement of the kingdom of God. Please contact Sermon on the Mount Publishing for permission before using it commercially or on the Internet. Brief quotations in reviews or articles are permitted.

ISBN 978-1-68001-001-5

Unless otherwise noted, Scripture taken from the New King James Version. Copyright © 1982 by Thomas Nelson, Inc. Used by permission. All rights reserved.

For more excellent titles, contact:
Sermon on the Mount Publishing
P.O. Box 246
Manchester, MI 48158
(734) 428-0488
the-witness@sbcglobal.net
www.kingdomreading.com

Our Mission:
To obey the commands of Christ and to teach men to do so.

First Printing—May 2014—1,716 copies
Second Printing—POD Edition

To Isaac and Melissa

Let it be understood that those who are not living by Christ's teachings are not Christians at all – even though they might profess His teachings with their lips.

—*Justin Martyr*

Contents

Acknowledgements	i
Foreword	iii
We Have a Problem	1
Russellisms	3
Magnifying Minors	7
Magnifying Theology	15
Magnifying Eschatology	21
Magnifying a Denomination	29
Magnifying a Bible Translation	35
Twisting Scripture	41
Pride	57
Wealth	65
Dishonesty with History	89
What Can We Learn from Jehovah's Witnesses?	99
What Jehovah's Witnesses Do Right!	119
The Gospel of the Kingdom	129
Come Holy Spirit	141
Challenge to the Nominal Christian	145
Illustration Credits	151

Acknowledgements

I thank my God upon every remembrance of you.
(Philippians 1:3)

I want to bless my dear wife, Tiffany, for her love, respect, and support. This book was inspired by my many conversations with her.

I also want to thank my brother Darren for his editorial work and helpful comments.

I'm indebted to the life-changing ministry of Scroll Publishing. Specifically, I want to thank Andre Bercot for his friendship and encouragement.

I owe a big thank you to Jennifer Burdge for her copy-editing work and Mike Atnip for page layout and cover design. I also want to thank Mike and John D. Martin for their love for Christ and their gift with the pen. A good portion of the words in this book came from them.

Finally, I want to acknowledge the Ste. Marie family. Thank you for your many hours of service you poured into this project. I could not have written this book without you.

There are many others I could mention.

~God bless you!

Foreword

Jehovah's Witnesses.

The term brings to mind pictures of people knocking on our doors, handing us Watchtower magazines, and wanting to have "Bible studies" in our homes – out of their own Bible translation, of course.

We all know the Jehovah's Witnesses are a cult, don't we?

But are most American churches really any different, in substance, from the Jehovah's Witnesses? Is it possible that the very things Jehovah's Witnesses do which we think of as wrong or unbalanced – such as magnifying (wrong) theology, magnifying minor and insignificant things, proclaiming false prophecies, magnifying eschatology, and twisting Scripture – are also hallmarks of much of professing American Christianity?

After becoming personally acquainted with the Jehovah's Witnesses, Matt Drayer is convinced that there are many parallels between the JWs and most of what is called "Christianity" in America today. He argues that the Jehovah's Witness system is simply another variation on the theme of popular American religion. This means that we in America – or wherever else we may find ourselves, because American/Western "Christianity" has influenced many areas of the world – need to examine ourselves carefully to discover whether or not we are guilty of any of these perversions of authentic, original Christianity, the Christianity taught by Jesus Christ and the Apostles.

Is Matt Drayer correct? Is Jehovah's Witness-ism simply another brand of a wrong system, the system of American Christianity? Does the church in America need to repent? Is true revival – a return to the life and faith of the New Testament – needed here in America? These questions I leave you, the reader, to answer, as you examine Brother Matt's work.

May the Lord add His blessing to this work, and may we all be challenged to magnify the Lord and be true Christians – not just "nominal" (in name only) Christians. To Him be all the glory!

~ Andrew V. Ste. Marie

Chapter 1

We Have a Problem

I would like you to think about heaven. Now, picture a small group of Christians chatting together in heaven. Pretend they just met and are taking turns sharing stories about their lives on earth. The first Christian to share was part of the early church. She was ripped apart by lions in the Coliseum. The next Christian shares about the horrors of communism. He was taken away from his family, imprisoned, tortured, and eventually killed for his faith in Christ. One by one, the Christians tell stories about persecution, pain, suffering, and martyrdom. Then the last Christian introduces himself and all mouths drop. After a period of silence, the others congratulate him with amazement.

Who was that last Christian? What was so special about him? Why was everybody so surprised to see him in heaven?

He was from America.

American Christianity

Greetings in the precious name of Jesus Christ. I have a deep concern for American Christianity. We say we are rich, and have become wealthy, and have need of nothing. I fear that we are wretched, miserable, poor, blind, and naked. I think that God will spit the American Church out of His mouth.

Many Americans are deceived. Yes, there are some true Christians in America. I'm sure there were some faithful Christians in Laodicea too. But for the most part, the Christianity of America is not true Christianity.

May I suggest that our problem is *Russellisms*?

Chapter 2

Russellisms

On February 16, 1852, a baby boy was born in Pennsylvania. His name was Charles Taze Russell. He was a bright little child with a lot of potential. His parents hoped he would grow up to be a mighty Christian. Unfortunately, Russell chose a totally different path. He ended up doing damage to Christianity.

Don't get me wrong: Russell was very interested in Christianity. The problem was that he was not interested in authentic Christianity. He wanted to make Christianity hold to everything that he believed.

Russell was determined. He studied the Bible, but was not willing to submit to it. He studied Christian history – to support his personal beliefs. He argued with various Christians. He even studied other religions. Eventually, he accomplished his goal . . . and a counterfeit Christianity was born.

Charles Taze Russell created a "Christianity" that was filled with all of his views, which I call Russellisms.

Starting a church

When Russell was only thirteen years old, he left his parents' church. Three years later, he walked away from church number two. Eventually, at the age of eighteen, he started his own church – a church where he could promote his Russellisms.

Russell was very successful. His church took off and is still going strong. They are called Jehovah's Witnesses. Today, there are millions of Jehovah's Witnesses all over the world. Perhaps one has even knocked on your door.

Meeting the Jehovah's Witnesses

A few years ago, before I knew about Russellisms, I developed a passion to converse with Jehovah's Witnesses. At the time, I didn't know anything about them except for the fact that all my friends called them a cult. I heard so many negative things about them that I decided to find out for myself what they actually believed. It usually takes my wife a while to join me in my passions, but once I had her support – I was off! They have a Kingdom Hall (meetinghouse) in my town, so I decided to drop in.

Charles Taze Russell (1852-1916)

I will always remember the day I nervously walked into their Kingdom Hall. It was not a Sunday, but there were some cars in the parking lot. I walked in and found some men having a Bible study. I apologized for interrupting and introduced myself. They were exceptionally cordial and welcomed me in. I asked them a few questions, and we decided to meet on a regular basis. We began meeting on Saturday mornings at my house. Occasionally, I would even attend their meetings. As time went on, I developed a nice relationship with them. I especially bonded with a Witness named Isaac. He and his wife would often drop by to say "Hello." Once they went on vacation and surprised us by bringing home gifts for our children.

After spending a few years with the Witnesses, I learned a lot. They are a sincere group of people trying to serve God the best way they know how. However, Jehovah's Witnesses are off base. They are not disciples of Jesus Christ. They are faithful disciples of Charles Russell, dogmatically proclaiming his Russellisms.

Making a discovery

After talking to Isaac one day, I decided to write down all the different Russellisms I observed among the Witnesses. As I did that, it hit me – Christians do the same things.

Many Christians are following the exact same list of Russellisms that the Witnesses are following. We will be discussing these Russellisms in the following chapters.

When I realized this, my passion changed. I still meet with the Witnesses, although my passion is no longer towards the Witnesses alone, but toward all those who unwittingly follow the ways of Charles Taze Russell.

That is why I wrote this book.

My prayer

I pray that my words come across in love and humility. I know that I'm going to step on a lot of toes. Please know that I am not judging anyone's eternal destination. I am not picking on any particular group or church. I have no denominational bias. I am just a man who desperately wants to see a revival of the New Testament church.

My desire is for Christians to get rid of their Russellisms.

Father in heaven, I am nothing. But if you can use a donkey to speak to a wayward prophet, then perhaps you can use me, weak as I am, to help bring revival. In Jesus' name, please use this book to touch and change the Christians in America. I pray that everyone will read with an open heart – especially the church leaders. Amen.

Chapter 3

Magnifying Minors

A wise grandpa once told me a story. He shared about a time his five-year-old grandson tried to catch a rabbit. At first, the rabbit was going east and his young grandson was in hot pursuit. Suddenly, the rabbit turned north while the oblivious boy continued traveling east. Thinking he was chasing the rabbit, he was actually getting further and further from it.

Jehovah's Witnesses think they are going in the right direction by magnifying a host of things that they feel are truly important. In reality, most of the things they magnify are minor, if not totally insignificant.

- They believe we must refer to God only by the name Jehovah.
- They claim that Jesus died on a torture stake instead of a cross.
- They will not obtain a blood transfusion.
- They don't celebrate birthdays.
- The list goes on.

Just like the little boy, they miss the point. They are going east while true Christianity is going north.

Christians do the same thing

When my wife and I were first married, we discovered that we had bees in our house. I'm not much of a handyman so we decided to call in an exterminator. After a few hours, a man showed up and took care of our bee problem. He was a talkative fellow. After he took care of the bees, I brought up the subject of Christianity and he told me that he was a Christian.[1] Then, to my disappointment, he began lecturing me about the correct pronunciation of Jesus' name. He said, "Christians are all pronouncing it wrong." He erroneously felt that a true Christian should not call Christ "Jesus," but should use the pronunciation from a different ancient language.

"Christians are all pronouncing it wrong."

Just like the Witnesses, Christians magnify all kinds of things that are minor points, or even totally insignificant.

The Sabbath

I was once walking through an industrial tent at a local fair. It was typical. The walls were lined with booths displaying products. Local businessmen were chatting with the people, inviting them to their booths, and trying to lure them in with popcorn. Then, I noticed something different. A church was using the industrial tent as an opportunity to evange-

---

1 Throughout this book, I am using the term "Christians" loosely, to refer to American professing Christians of non-Jehovah's Witness type.

lize. I thought that was a great idea, so I decided to walk over and give them some encouragement. As I approached their booth, I quickly discovered that they were Seventh Day Adventists. I struck up a conversation with them and they aggressively told me that Christians need to keep the Jewish Sabbath. We talked a while, but I eventually gave up. I left that conversation very discouraged.

The Sabbath was for Old Testament Jews. It is not a requirement for New Testament Christians.

Facial hair

In 1832, a zealous young Christian named Samuel Froehlich (1803-1857) began a revival of New Testament Christianity in Switzerland. He started a church that became known as The Apostolic Christian Church of America. Although Switzerland constantly persecuted him, Froehlich didn't back down. Through diligent evangelism, his church spread throughout Europe and into America.

Unfortunately, about fifty years after Froehlich passed away, his church was torn apart by a mustache. A problem arose between the Eastern Europeans and Western Europeans that settled in America. The men from Eastern Europe had beards and mustaches, while the men from Western Europe had beards with no mustaches. The Christians from Western Europe would not fellowship with the Christians from Eastern Europe unless they agreed to shave off their mustaches. The Christians from Eastern Europe refused. It led to a national church split.

I read some of the documents about this split. It was unbelievable (bitter feuds, angry words, crying wives, even excommunication) . . . and all because of a mustache. A mustache!

Sadly, that is not the end of the story. You would think they would realize how silly it is to make such a big deal about facial hair. Nope. To this day, members of the Apostolic Christian Church of America are not allowed to have any facial hair at all.

The list goes on

Pentecostals magnify (what they call) speaking in tongues. I don't deny the biblical gift of tongues, and I'm sure some Christians speak in tongues today, but it is not essential for every Christian.

- Some Christians magnify a particular mode of baptism.
- Some magnify a health and wealth gospel (which is the opposite of what Jesus taught).
- Some magnify "healings."
- Some magnify church traditions.
- Some magnify Praise and Worship music.
- Some magnify a person.
- Some even magnify health food.

The Catholic Church probably takes the crown for magnifying the largest number of minor, insignificant, and unbiblical things, such as Mary's perpetual virginity, prayers to the saints, apostolic succession, holy water, clerical celibacy, penance, etc.

JESUS should be magnified

Instead of minimizing Jesus with all our inconsequential tangents, we should be magnifying Him! He is our Savior, Redeemer, Lord, and King. Why would we magnify anything or anyone else?

Eric Ludy brilliantly calls Jesus our "North Star." Amen! Christians should be universally magnifying the North Star. Jesus should be the main subject of every church. Jesus, Jesus, Jesus!

Origen (185-254 A.D.) wrote:

> I hope to be addressed not by the name of some heresiarch [originator of heresy], but by the name of Christ. I hope to have his name, which is blessed upon the earth. I desire, both in deed and in thought, both to be and to be called a Christian.[2]

Paul said, "I am jealous for you with godly jealousy. For I have betrothed you to one husband, that I may present you as a chaste virgin to Christ. But I fear, lest somehow, as the serpent deceived Eve by his craftiness, so your minds may be corrupted from the simplicity that is in Christ" (II Corinthians 11:2-3).

What does it mean to magnify Jesus?

> *"And I, if I am lifted up from the earth, will draw all peoples to Myself"* (John 12:32).

Let's get practical.

Christians who truly magnify Jesus are disciples of Jesus. Oswald Chambers said, "The New Testament example of the Christian experience is that of a personal, passionate devotion to the Person of Jesus Christ."[3]

Webster's 1828 Dictionary defines a Christian this way: "A real disciple of Christ; one who believes in the truth of the Christian religion, and studies to follow the example, and

---

2 Origen, *Homilies in Luke* 16.6, as cited in Thomas P. Scheck (translator), *Origen: Commentary on the Epistle to the Romans Books 1-5*, 2001, Catholic University of America Press, p. 319.
3 Oswald Chambers, *My Utmost for His Highest*, 1992, Discovery House Publishers, November 29.

obey the precepts, of Christ; a believer in Christ who is characterized by real piety."

The Bible says that Christians are people who live just like Jesus lived (I John 2:6). They love God like Christ loved God. They hate sin like Christ hated sin. They pray like Christ prayed. They treat others like Christ treated others.

It is very simple: Christians are just like Christ. They have a relationship with Him. They have Christ's character inside them. They love Him, AND they obey Him.

Jesus said, "He who has My commandments and keeps them, it is he who loves Me. And he who loves Me will be loved by My Father, and I will love him and manifest Myself to him" (John 14:21).

A beautiful example

We experienced a tragedy in our community in early 2012. An Amish family was blissfully traveling down a road in their horse and buggy when a young man in a full size van accidentally hit them. Horrified, the man called 911 on his cell phone and an ambulance was immediately summoned. The mother of the Amish family was in critical condition, but survived. Three children died.

A lot of tears were shed that day.

However, the devastation of death was erased by what happened next. The Amish father completely forgave the man who killed his children. He held no bitterness. The only thing he held was his wife's hand while she rested on the hospital bed. There were no angry words at the funeral. No threat of suing. The Amish showed only love and forgiveness.

The community was stunned. However, the Amish weren't doing anything radical. They were simply magnifying Jesus Christ.

Jesus said (as they crucified Him), "Father forgive them, for they do not know what they do" (Luke 23:34).

"For if you forgive men their trespasses, your heavenly Father will also forgive you. But if you do not forgive men their trespasses, neither will your Father forgive your trespasses" (Matthew 6:14-15).

That Amish family beautifully demonstrated what normal Christianity is supposed to look like when we magnify Jesus.

Oh come let us adore Him,
Oh come let us adore Him,
Oh come let us adore Him, Christ the Lord.

Chapter 4

Magnifying Theology

To Jehovah's Witnesses, a Christian is somebody who has all the "right" knowledge.

Witnesses hold up theology like it was the most important thing that Christ taught. They believe they are the true church because they are the only ones who have all their theological ducks in a row. Ironically, some of their theology is way off.[4]

Christians do the same thing

Once upon a time, a man was arrested for committing numerous crimes. He found himself staring at a judge and facing life behind bars. The man admitted to the crimes but didn't think he deserved to go to jail. The judge was confused and asked him to explain himself. With a look of confidence, the man said, "Your honor, I know where you live. I know your hobbies and your food preferences. I know you have a dog, four cats, and a goldfish. Your wife's name is Maggie

---

[4] Jehovah's Witnesses hold to a position called Arianism, a heretical teaching that has been around for centuries. Arianism claims that Jesus is not of the same substance as God and was created out of nothing. Jehovah's Witnesses also do not believe that humans have souls.

and you have three children. You see, your honor, I know all about you. Therefore, you can't possibly send me to jail."

As ridiculous as this story is, many Christians believe Christianity works that way. They think God will ignore your sins and pat you on the back if you have the correct head knowledge.

Head knowledge versus obedience

There are many Christians who know what the Bible says. They can tell you all about Jesus and explain the plan of salvation. They might even have some Bible verses memorized. But they are not disciples of Christ.

There are also many Christians who study the Bible. They seek to grasp every area of theology. Some of them go to college to further educate themselves. They can tell you all about hermeneutics and anthropomorphism. They may even become ministers. But they are not disciples of Christ.

I'm sure King Saul knew the Scriptures.

There is a big difference between somebody who knows the Bible and somebody who knows the Author of the Bible. There is a big difference between somebody who studies the Bible for theological purposes and somebody who studies the Bible because he loves God. I'm sure King Saul knew the Scriptures. So did Korah, Achan, Uzzah, Nadab, and Abihu. These were all prominent Israelite men.

However, these men didn't obey God, and they all ended up dead.

A true Christian obeys God's Word. Yes, he will have head knowledge (because God wants us to embrace His Word). But God's desire is not for Christians to have *just* head knowledge. Scripture says, "But be doers of the word, and not hearers only, deceiving yourselves" (James 1:22).

Leonard Ravenhill said, "One of these days some simple soul will pick up the Book of God, read it, and believe it. Then the rest of us will be embarrassed. We have adopted the convenient theory that the Bible is a book to be explained, whereas first and foremost it is a book to be believed (and after that to be obeyed)."[5]

"Great" preachers

Many Christians lift up preachers who are educated, intelligent, entertaining, and popular. These Christians are impressed by seminary-trained theologians who can wax eloquent and expound on deep subjects. They applaud preachers who use elongated words and swoon when the speakers say something in Greek.

Is that the kind of preacher Jesus was? What about Paul, Peter, or any of the Apostles?

Paul said, "And I brethren, when I came to you, did not come with excellence of speech or of wisdom declaring to you the testimony of God. For I determined not to know anything among you except Jesus Christ and Him crucified. I was with you in weakness, in fear, and in much trembling. And my speech and my preaching were not with persuasive words of human wisdom, but in demonstration of the Spirit

---

5   Leonard Ravenhill, *Why Revival Tarries*, 1987, Bethany House Publishers, p. 71.

Great preachers are Christ-like examples who help others become more like Jesus. Anabaptist minister Pieter Pietersz preaches at a secret meeting in a boat.

and of power, that your faith should not be in the wisdom of men but in the power of God" (I Corinthians 2:1-5).

Don't lift up the wisdom of men. I'm not against preachers who can explain theology, but theology should never be elevated above Christ-centered living. Great preachers aren't people who flaunt a bunch of educated fluff. They are Christ-like examples who help others become more like Jesus.

Paul clearly explains this when he lists the qualifications of an elder/bishop. He said, "If a man is blameless, the husband of one wife, having faithful children not accused of dissipation [debauchery] or insubordination [disobedience]. For a bishop must be blameless, as a steward of God, not self-willed, not quick tempered, not given to wine, not violent, not greedy for money, but hospitable, a lover of what is good, sober-minded, just, holy, and self-controlled, holding fast the faithful word as he has been taught, that he may be able, by sound doctrine, both to exhort and convict those who contradict" (Titus 1:6-9).

Dividing the body

"For where there are envy, strife, and divisions among you, are you not carnal and behaving like mere men?" (I Corinthians 3:3).

Christians who magnify theology tend to divide the body of Christ. They make a big deal about minor differences and argue about things that nobody really understands. They pick sides, lift up their views, and belittle anybody who thinks differently.

Don't split hairs and separate over theological beliefs. All the head knowledge that is really needed is contained in the Apostle's Creed:

> I believe in God the Father Almighty, Creator of heaven and earth; and in Jesus Christ, His only Son, our Lord, who was conceived by the Holy Spirit, born of the Virgin Mary, suffered under Pontius Pilate, was crucified, died, and was buried. He descended into hades, on the third day He rose again from the dead. He ascended into heaven, and sits on the right hand of God the Father Almighty. From there He shall come to judge the living and the dead. I believe in the Holy Spirit, the holy catholic [or universal] church, the communion of saints, the forgiveness of sins, the resurrection of the body, and the life everlasting.

If you want to go beyond the Apostle's Creed, that is fine. Personally, I enjoy a good discussion about angels, demons, the Trinity, life after death, etc. However, these things should be discussed with love and openness. Humbly consider the opinions of others and serve Christ together.

One last thing: I want to encourage everyone to get rid of two labels: "Calvinist" and "Arminian." Those two words have caused much division to Christianity. Can't we be disciples of the Lord Jesus Christ, first and only?

Zach

I want to finish this chapter by telling you about Zach. Zach is no longer with us because he died of cancer on June 6, 2013, but I was privileged to be one of his closest friends. We had many late night theological discussions together. He was very intelligent and studious in the Scriptures. But that is not why he is remembered. Few people knew that he liked theology. He is remembered for being a faithful disciple of Christ. He is remembered for knowing the Bible, but he is better remembered for obeying the Bible.

Zach talked about Jesus and lived like Jesus. He loved God and hated sin. He had a deep prayer life. He was a wonderful husband and father. He loved everyone he met. He was kind, joyful, and enthusiastic. He was respected in the community for his integrity and his acts of service. The last three years of his life were dedicated to helping orphans in Haiti.

This should be the testimony of every Christian, with or without a terminal disease.

"If anyone desires to come after Me, let him deny himself, and take up his cross daily, and follow Me. For whoever desires to save his life will lose it, but whoever loses his life for My sake will save it." –*Jesus*

Chapter 5

Magnifying Eschatology

Jesus said, "Watch therefore, for you do not know what hour your Lord is coming" (Matthew 24:42).

Apparently, Charles Russell took those words as a challenge. He tried to prove Jesus wrong. In the late 1800s, he announced that the end of the world would come in 1914. He said the following:

Armageddon will end

"... The battle of the great day of God Almighty ... The date of the close of that 'battle' is definitely marked in Scripture as October 1914. It is already in progress, its beginning dating from October, 1874."[6]

Times of trouble will end

"The seventh trumpet sounds from Aug. 1840, until 'the time of trouble,' or day of wrath is ended. Hence, it doubtless ends with the times of the Gentiles, and this forty years of conquest; and therefore, sounds until A. D. 1914; at the end of which, Babylon the great, will have fallen, and the

---

[6] *Zion's Watch Tower*, January 15, 1892, p. 23.

'dragon' be bound: that is, the nations will be subdued, and 'the prince of this world cast out.'"[7]

"... Our readers are writing to know if there may not be a mistake in the 1914 date. They do not see how present conditions can hold out so long under the strain. We see no reason for changing the figures – nor could we change them if we would. They are, we believe, God's dates, not ours. But bear in mind that the end of 1914 is not the date for the beginning, but for the end of the time of trouble."[8]

False religions will end

"A.D. 33, to A.D. 70 was 36 ½ years; and so from A.D. 1878 to the end of A.D. 1914 is 36 ½ years. And, with the end of A.D. 1914, what God calls Babylon, and what men call Christendom, will have passed away, as already shown in prophecy."[9]

"October, 1914, will witness the full end of Babylon, 'as a great millstone cast into the sea,' utterly destroyed as a system."[10]

Governments will be overthrown

"True, it is expecting great things to claim, as we do, that within the coming twenty-six years all present governments will be overthrown and dissolved. In view of this strong Bible evidence concerning the Times of the Gentiles, we consider it an established truth that the final end of the kingdoms of this world, and the full establishment of the Kingdom of God, will be accomplished at the end of A. D. 1914. Be not surprised, then, when in subsequent chapters we present

---

7   *Three Worlds and the Harvest of This World* 1877, Barbour & Russell, p. 27.
8   *Zion's Watch Tower*, July 15, 1894, p. 226.
9   *Studies in the Scriptures - Thy Kingdom Come*, 1891, p. 153.
10 *Watch Tower*, June 15, 1911, p. 190.

proofs that the setting up of the Kingdom of God is already begun, that it is pointed out in prophecy as due to begin the exercise of power in A.D. 1878, and that the 'battle of the great day of God Almighty' (Rev. 16:14), which will end in A.D. 1914 with the complete overthrow of earth's present rulership, is already commenced. The gathering of the armies is plainly visible from the standpoint of God's Word."[11]

"We have seen that God has a set time for every feature of his plan, and that we are even now in this 'Day of Vengeance,' which is a period of forty years; that it began in October, 1874, and will end in October, 1914 [very shortly]."[12]

Jesus will begin ruling the earth

"Not until the full end of Gentile Times (October, A.D. 1914) should we expect the earthly phase of God's Kingdom; for in giving a lease of dominion to the Gentiles until that date God made no mistake and his plans alter not. The earthly phase of the Kingdom of God when set up will be Israelitish; for such is God's engagement or covenant with Abraham and his natural seed. Even the chief favor, the spiritual Kingdom, was offered first to fleshly Israel, and would have been given to them if they had been ready at heart to receive it on the conditions attached to it – to suffer with Christ and afterward to be glorified with him."[13]

The resurrection will occur

"And yet 'Jerusalem must be trodden down of the Gentiles, until the times of the Gentiles are fulfilled;' hence, trodden

---

11 *Studies in the Scriptures Series II - The Time Is At Hand*, 1889, pp. 99, 101.
12 *Studies in the Scriptures Series IV - The Day of Vengeance*, 1897, pp. 546, 547.
13 *Studies in the Scriptures Series IV - The Day of Vengeance*, 1897, pp. 624, 625.

down until A. D. 1914, when the day of wrath will be passed, and the resurrection and return of the 'whole house of Israel' due."[14]

"The beginning of the earthly phase of the Kingdom in the end of A.D. 1914 will, we understand, consist wholly of the resurrected holy ones of olden time–from John the Baptizer back to Abel – 'Abraham, Isaac, Jacob and all the holy prophets.'"[15]

The 144,000 will all be in heaven

"That the deliverance of the saints must take place sometime before 1914 is manifest, since the deliverance of fleshly Israel, as we shall see, is appointed to take place at that time . . . . just how long before 1914 the last living members of the body of Christ will be glorified, we are not directly informed."[16, 17]

Christians do the same thing

The year 1914 came and went. Russell was a false prophet. Surprisingly, that did not stop the Witnesses. They just changed their story, covered up Russell's false prophesies, and continued making predictions:

1918, 1920, 1925, 1941, 1957, 1975, 1984, and 1994.[18]

Sadly, Christians do it too.

Here are just a few examples:

The year 1000 goes down as one of the most pronounced states of hysteria over the return of Christ. All members of society seemed affected by the prediction that Jesus was

---

14 *Three Worlds and The Harvest of This World*, 1877, p.166.
15 *Studies in the Scriptures Series IV - The Day of Vengeance*, 1897, p. 625.
16 *Studies in the Scriptures - Thy Kingdom Come*, 1908 edition, p. 228.
17 All Russell quotes as cited by "1914: Failed Watchtower Prophecy," www.jwfacts.com (Accessed July 22, 2013).
18 *Pre Date Setters*, www.bible.ca (Accessed July 22, 2013).

coming back on January 1, 1000 AD. There really weren't any of the events required by the Bible transpiring at that time. The magical number 1000 was primarily the sole reason for the expectation. During December 999 AD, everyone was on their best behavior; worldly goods were sold and given to the poor, swarms of pilgrims headed east to meet the Lord at Jerusalem, buildings went unrepaired, crops were left unplanted, and criminals were set free from jails.[19]

The year 2000 was also a big scare. I find it interesting however, that instead of giving away goods, people were hoarding them, in fear of a technological crisis.

In the 16th century, a man named Thomas Müntzer, a leader in the German Peasant's Rebellion, announced that the return of Christ was near. He believed the Lord would return after he and his men destroyed the high and mighty. This belief led to an uneven battle with government troops where he was strategically out-numbered. Müntzer claimed to have a vision from God in which the Lord promised that He would catch the cannon balls of the enemy in the sleeves of His cloak. The vision turned out

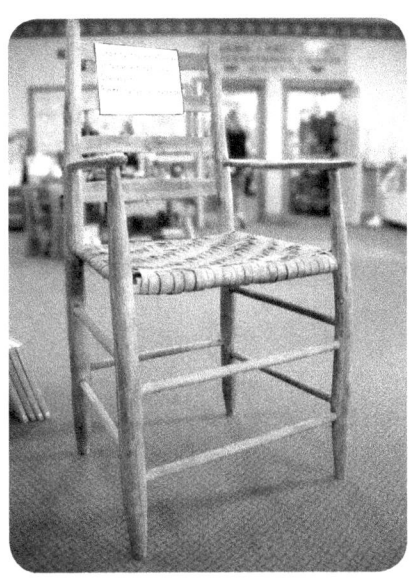

Jonas Stutzman was so convinced that Christ would return in 1853 that he built a chair for Him to sit in.

---
19   *Ibid.*

to be false when Müntzer's followers were mowed down by cannon fire.[20] Müntzer was arrested and beheaded.

William Miller was the founder of an end-times movement that was so prominent it received its own name—Millerism. From his studies of the Bible, Miller determined that the second coming would happen sometime between 1843 and 1844. A spectacular meteor shower in 1833 gave the movement a good push forward. The buildup of anticipation continued until March 21, 1844, when Miller's one year time table ran out. Some followers set another date of October 22, 1844. This too failed.[21]

Ellen G. White, founder of the Seventh Day Adventists, made many predictions regarding the timing of the end of the world. All failed. In her last prediction she said that she was shown in a vision the fate of believers who attended the 1856 Seventh Day Adventists conference. She wrote "Some of the attendees would die of normal diseases; some would die from plagues at the last days, others would still be alive when Jesus comes back." By the early 1900s, all those who attended the conference had passed away.

An Amish man named Jonas Stutzman (from Holmes County, Ohio) predicted that Christ would return in 1853. He was so convinced that he built a chair for Christ to sit in. This chair can be seen at the Behalt Museum in Berlin, Ohio.

The book *88 Reasons Why the Rapture is in 1988* came out only a few months before the event was to take place. What little time the book had, it used effectively. By the time September 11-13 rolled around, whole churches were caught up in the excitement the book generated.[22]

A year later, Edgar Whisenaunt, author of *88 Reasons Why the Rapture is in 1988*, came out with a new book called

---

20   *Ibid.*
21   *Ibid.*
22   *Ibid.*

89 Reasons why the Rapture is in 1989. This book was not as popular.

We don't know!

In 1809, a fortune teller named Mary Bateman had a magic hen that laid eggs with end time messages on them. One message said that Christ was coming. You can imagine the uproar it created. However, the uproar ended when an unannounced visitor caught Mary forcing an egg into her "magic" hen's oviduct.[23]

Mary Bateman claimed that she had a magic hen that laid eggs with end time messages on them.

That is laughable, isn't it? Well, Christians who make false predictions about Christ's return look just as foolish.

A few years ago, I was driving down the road and saw an unusual billboard that read, "May 21, 2011: Judgment Day." I came to find out that a man named Harold Camping was adamantly claiming that he knew when Christ would return and was proclaiming his prophesy on billboards all over the country. He was wrong, and Christianity suffered another embarrassing wound.

---

23 *Ibid.*

"Watch"

We know very little about the end times. If you want to study eschatology, that is fine. Just don't get dogmatic about your views. You just might be wrong. And please, PLEASE, do not try to predict when Christ will return.

Mark Twain said, "Most people are bothered by those passages of Scripture they don't understand, but for me I have always noticed that the passages that bother me are those I do understand."[24] Mark Twain wasn't even a Christian, but every Christian should have this perspective. Don't get hung up and divided over parts of Scripture that are unclear. Faithfully submit to the Scriptures that are clear and serve Christ faithfully until He comes back.

Jesus sums it up well in Mark 13:32-37. He said, "But of that day and hour no one knows, not even the angels in heaven, nor the Son, but only the Father. Take heed, watch and pray; for you do not know when the time is. *It is* like a man going to a far country, who left his house and gave authority to his servants, and to each his work, and commanded the doorkeeper to watch. Watch therefore, for you do not know when the master of the house is coming—in the evening, at midnight, at the crowing of the rooster, or in the morning—lest, coming suddenly, he find you sleeping. And what I say to you, I say to all: Watch!"

---

24 As cited in Ray Comfort, ed., *The Evidence Bible*, 2003, Bridge-Logos Publishers, p. 1189.

Chapter 6

Magnifying a Denomination

All the children at Ossian elementary were eagerly anticipating the last day of school. It was a day of fun, food, activities, and races. The main attraction was an annual race for the boys. The winner of this race was declared the fastest boy in the school. This particular year, a scrappy young farm boy named Tim was planning on winning. The day finally came. When it was time for the big race, everybody came to watch. The fastest boys came over and lined up. Tim was ready. All was quiet until the judge shouted "Go!" The boys took off and zoomed towards the finish line. Tim ran as fast as he could and soon got ahead of the pack. There was only one boy close to him when he crossed the finish line. Everybody cheered! He did it! Tim was the fastest boy in the whole school. As the smoke cleared, the judge walked towards the sweaty runners to award the winner. Tim gleefully held out his hand to receive his first-place ribbon. However, his happiness turned into disappointment and confusion when the judge passed him and handed the ribbon to the second place finisher. The crowd gasped. Tim questioned the judge's decision, and the judge said, "Sorry young man. But I believe this boy was the winner." Tim was crushed. He sadly trudged away holding a second-place ribbon. Meanwhile, the "winner" walked over to the judge and said two words that explained everything:

"Thanks, Dad!"

Humans are naturally biased towards people they love. Sometimes, their bias trumps reality. In this incident, a judge gave his son an undeserved trophy. I'm sure that everyone reading this is screaming for justice. Well, calm down. It was just a silly race. Tim survived. A much bigger problem is when Christians allow their bias to trump God's Word.

I love my wife and children dearly. I have the best parents in the world. I am very thankful for all my friends, family, and in-laws. Our loved ones are a blessing from God. However, they become a curse if we put them above God. Truthfully (and sadly), there are many Christians who change their minds about sin when it comes close to home. For example, many Christians accept homosexuality if they know somebody who is a homosexual. Many Christians accept divorce and remarriage when somebody in their family goes through it. I see it all the time. Instead of being steadfast, Christians become moved by their emotional bias and excuse sin. Scripture says, "Do not be deceived. Neither fornicators, nor idolaters, nor adulterers, nor homosexuals, nor sodomites, nor thieves, nor covetous, nor drunkards, nor revilers, nor extortioners will inherit the kingdom of God" (I Corinthians 6:9-10).

I say all this to reveal how easily we can put things above God. This brings us to the next Russellism. Jehovah's Witnesses put their denomination above God. They believe they are the only true church. They condemn anybody who is not a Jehovah's Witness. They are not even allowed to attend another church.

The Witnesses claim to be exalting Jehovah. Actually, they are exalting their organization.

Christians do the same thing

I want to briefly stress how Scriptural (and vital) it is for Christians to be a part of a church. Some people want to be Christians without any church affiliation. These Christians experience no baptism, no discipleship, no accountability, no fellowship – and no Christianity. Every Christian should be part of a church or seeking a church.

On the other hand! Christians can go too far, like the Witnesses, and magnify their church. There is a word for that. It is called idolatry.

Christ is the head

The story is told that John Wesley had a dream in which he was ushered to the gates of heaven. He asked, "Are there any Presbyterians here?" The answer came back, "No." He asked, "Are there any Baptists?" "No." "Are there any Catholics, Lutherans, Anabaptists, or Methodists?" Each time the answer was "No." To this, Wesley asked, "Who then is inside?" The answer came back, "All those who love the Lord."

The church is a body. Scripture says, "There is one body" (Ephesians 4:4). This body is made up of men and women all over the world that love the Lord. They are the hands and feet of Jesus. Obviously, this body cannot all meet together in one huge building, so it is divided up into countless local bodies that are interspersed throughout the earth. This is the way it has always been. Paul told the Christians in Rome, "All the churches of Christ greet you" (Romans 16:16). Though churches are separated by miles, different languages, and different cultures, they all have one big thing in common – Jesus Christ. "He is the head of the body, the church" (Colossians 1:18).

Unfortunately, many Christians cut off their head (Jesus) and emphasize their particular church body. They love their church more than they love Christ. They lift up their church. Their church becomes the focus. Their church does everything right. Their church is better than other churches. Their church, their church, their church...

We cannot put the church above Christ. This creates religious church-goers (who usually end up persecuting the true Christians). Jesus said, "He who loves father or mother more than Me is not worthy of Me. And he who loves son or daughter more than Me is not worthy of Me" (Matthew 10:37). What about, "He who loves his church more than Me is not worthy of Me?"

I will never forget the time I helped my grandfather butcher chickens. It was quite traumatizing. The first thing we had to do was kill the chicken. To do this, Grandpa would chop their heads off with an ax. To my amazement, the chickens would actually run around for a while. However, they would always fall over dead eventually. They couldn't survive without their head. Neither can the church. We need to stay focused on Christ.

Always remember: the biggest opponents of Jesus were religious people.

Christ is the Way

Jesus said, "I am the way, the truth, and the life. No one comes to the Father except through Me" (John 14:6).

Some people think their church will take them to heaven. That is not how it works. Going to church doesn't make you a Christian. Somebody once said, "Going to church doesn't make you any more a Christian than going to the garage makes you a car."

Leonard Ravenhill said, "Had Saul met only a preacher and heard only a sermon on the Damascus road, he might never have been heard of again. But he met Christ!"[25]

A Christian is somebody who has personally met Jesus Christ. Jesus said, "I am the door. If anyone enters by **Me**, he will be saved" (John 10:9).

Christ is the Truth

"For the law was given through Moses, but grace and truth came through Jesus Christ" (John 1:17).

Some churches call Jesus "Lord" but they don't obey Him (Luke 6:46). These churches are neglecting their responsibility and leading people astray. Jesus said, "Enter by the narrow gate; for wide is the gate and broad is the way that leads to destruction, and there are many who go in by it. Because narrow is the gate and difficult is the way which leads to life, and there are few who find it" (Matthew 7:13-14).

On the day of Pentecost, "those who gladly received (Peter's) word were baptized; and that day about three thousand souls were added to them. And they continued steadfastly in the apostle's doctrine and fellowship, in the breaking of bread, and in prayers" (Acts 2:41-42). 2,000 years later, the church's job is still the same – to continue steadfastly in the doctrine (teachings) of Jesus and His apostles.

Christ is the Life

The Apostle John said, "He who has the Son has life; he who does not have the Son of God does not have life" (I John 5:12).

Churches are full of life. They have lots of organization, attractive church buildings, huge gymnasiums, entertaining

---
25 Leonard Ravenhill, *Why Revival Tarries*, 1987, Bethany House Publishers, p. 117.

programs, loud music, eloquent preachers, flashy church signs, and activities for all ages . . . but is this the "life" that John was talking about? Whatever happened to the Holy Ghost? Whatever happened to prayer, power, miracles, suffering, persecution, and the peace which surpasses all understanding?

Scripture says, "And when they had prayed, the place where they were assembled together was shaken; and they were all filled with the Holy Spirit, and they spoke the word of God with boldness" (Acts 4:31).

"…And when they had called for the apostles and beaten them, they commanded that they should not speak in the name of Jesus, and let them go. So they departed from the presence of the council, rejoicing that they were counted worthy to suffer shame for His name. And daily in the temple, and in every house, they did not cease teaching and preaching Jesus as the Christ" (Acts 5:40-42).

"And when they had laid many stripes on them, they threw them into prison, commanding the jailer to keep them securely. Having received such a charge, he put them into the inner prison and fastened their feet in the stocks. But at midnight Paul and Silas were praying and singing hymns to God, and the prisoners were listening to them. Suddenly, there was a great earthquake" (Acts 16:23-26).

I think there is much more to church than what we are experiencing in America.

Chapter 7

Magnifying a Bible Translation

*I*n 1961, the Jehovah's Witnesses produced a Bible translation called the New World Translation of the Holy Scriptures (NWT). The translators said:

> The translators of this work, who fear and love the Divine author of the Holy Scriptures, feel toward Him a special responsibility to transmit his thoughts and declarations as accurately as possible. They also feel a responsibility toward the searching readers who depend upon a translation of the inspired Word of the Most High God for their everlasting salvation.[26]

That sounds really nice. But in reality, the NWT is flooded with Jehovah's Witness dogma:

- It uses the name Jehovah 6,973 times in the Old Testament and 237 times in the New.[27]
- It never uses the word "cross." For example, Mark 15:29-30 says, "And those going by would speak

---
26   *New World Translation of the Holy Scriptures,* 1984, Watchtower Bible and Tract Society of New York, Foreword.
27   The name Jehovah never appears in the Greek text of the New Testament.

abusively to him, wagging their heads and saying, 'Bah! You would-be-thrower-down of the temple and builder of it in three days' time, save yourself by coming down off the *torture stake*'" (NWT, emphasis mine).

- The biggest liberty they take is in their translation of John 1:1 – "In the beginning the Word was, and the Word was with God, and the Word was a god." This was not an honest translation from the Greek. It was translated this way to push their Arian agenda.

Regardless, Jehovah's Witnesses magnify their Bible. They think they are the only ones who are "truly" reading God's Word.

Christians do the same thing

Not all Christians magnify a translation. Some magnify a language.

God is not partial to a particular language. His desire is for people to read His Word in a language that they can understand. Unfortunately, humans tend to get caught up in a misconception. They think the Bible has to be written in a specific "holy language."

This misconception has plagued Christianity for centuries.

William Tyndale (c. 1494-1536), the first man to translate the entire New Testament from Greek into English. Photo on next page is a sample of his work.

Three European criminals

In 1384, a man named John Wycliffe passed away. About four decades later, Pope Martin V ordered his body to be dug up, burned, and thrown into a river.

John Huss promoted Wycliffe's ideas. He was burned at the stake in 1415 by the Roman Catholic Church.

In 1490, William Tyndale was born. He shared the same vision as Wycliffe and Huss. In 1535, he was arrested and imprisoned in the castle of Vilvoorden where he lived in awful conditions for over 500 days. On October 6, 1536, Tyndale was strangled and burned at the stake. His last words were, "Lord! Open the king of England's eyes."

What was their crime?

"Heresy!"

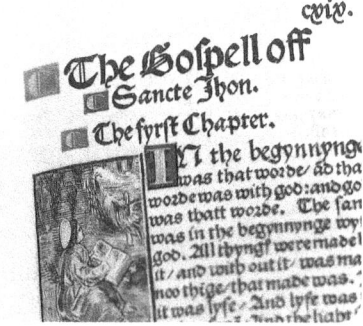

During the Protestant Reformation, Bibles were finally translated into modern languages.

"Holy languages"

At the close of the fourth century, the church wanted to have a universal Bible. The main language was Latin, so they had the Bible translated into the Latin language by a man named Jerome. Although there were already Latin Bibles, Jerome's translation (the Latin Vulgate) became the chosen translation. In time, the Vulgate became "the only Bible," and Latin became God's "holy language." As years went by, the vast majority of the people did not speak Latin, though it was studied by priests and scholars. Thus, the common person could not read the Bible.

Praise God, men like Wycliffe and Tyndale came along. These "heretics" wanted to translate the Bible into the common language of the people. They faced resistance, persecution, and torture from the church; but they didn't back down. And they did not die in vain! During the Protestant Reformation, Bibles were finally translated into modern languages.

Sadly, the battle still continues.

In some churches, God's "holy language" is German. I could take you to an Amish community just a few miles from my house where the German Bible is magnified. The Amish in this community speak two languages: English and a form of Swiss that is influenced by English. They do not fluently speak German. Therefore, most of them cannot read the very Bible they magnify.

I was once visiting with an elderly lady who was a member of a church that switched from German to English. She said, "I will always remember the first time I heard a sermon in English. I got goose bumps . . . because I could actually understand what the preacher was saying!"

Wow. Those Catholics and Amish sure are silly aren't they? Latin, German, God's language? Oh brother. Well, don't point too many fingers. I need to bring up one more holy language. There are scores of Christians who think that God's "holy language" is English. Not modern English, but the English that was spoken 400 years ago.

The King James Bible was written in 1611 (slightly updated in 1769). The English language has changed a lot since then, but KJV-only proponents believe God's word cannot be written in modern English. I once saw a bumper sticker that said, "If it ain't the King James, it ain't the Bible." Yikes! If Wycliffe, Huss, and Tyndale were alive today, who knows what the KJV-only proponents would do to them?

There is no holy language

I repeat: God's desire is for people to read His word in a language that they can understand. There are hundreds of different Bible translations in the English language (we should be thankful). I am not bashing the KJV; I am making a plea to the KJV-only crowd to stop using faulty arguments to push their version on other people. There is nothing uniquely inspired or holy about the King James Version.

Don't pick a version and magnify it. Pick a version and humbly submit to what it says.

Bryce Geiser wrote:

> Our problem today is not that we have too many Bible translations. No, the problem is that too many people do not obey the one they are reading.[28]

Obviously, we need to use discernment. There may be times when translators stray from the original text. For example, the Holy Spirit said, "Greet all the brethren with a holy kiss" (I Thessalonians 5:26), but the J.B. Phillips New Testament says, "Give a handshake all round among the brotherhood." J.B. Phillips took the words "holy kiss" out of the Bible. Translators are not always perfect. Sometimes they make innocent mistakes and sometimes they let their bias slip in.

I need to mention one translation that is an outright abomination – the Queen James Version. This "translation" was published in 2012 to promote the homosexual lifestyle. I agree with Ken Ham, who said:

> These people who have mutilated God's Word for their own anti-God agenda will have to answer to God for that one day—and there will be a day of

---

[28] Bryce Geiser, "An Anabaptist Looks at Bible Versions," *Plain Things* 1(5) (September/October 2013), p. 21. Caneyville Christian Community, 1000 Choncie Lee Road, Caneyville, KY 42721.

reckoning! I couldn't imagine standing before the Creator God and saying, "I hope you liked how we rewrote your holy Word. We just felt like those verses about homosexual behavior were unfair and outdated. We knew better than you did, and you obviously didn't want us to trust you in this area.[29]

Matthew and Mitchell

Matthew and Mitchell are cousins. They are almost exactly the same age, born a week apart. They were very close friends growing up and their families went to the same church.

Mitchell had a rough childhood. His parents got a divorce when he was in elementary school and he pretty much never saw his father again. He eventually stopped going to church. Matthew, on the other hand, kept going to church and became a Christian at the age of nineteen. Shortly after becoming a Christian, Matthew had an opportunity to go on a work team to Jamaica for a week. To his surprise, Mitchell decided to go as well.

One day in Jamaica, Matthew noticed that Mitchell was reading a Bible! Was he excited? Did he encourage him? Did he strike up a conversation? Did he ask him what he was reading? Did he ask him how he was doing spiritually?

Nope. Matthew got mad at Mitchell and unsympathetically admonished him for reading a Bible that was not a King James Version.

With shame, I confess that this story is about me. I am Matthew. I used to worship the KJV. I had the same attitude as the bumper sticker ("If it ain't the King James, it ain't the Bible"). I am thankful God is patient. It took a few years, but He eventually opened my eyes.

---

[29] Ken Ham, "Now it's the Queen James Bible," blogs.answersingenesis.org (Accessed July 15, 2013).

Chapter 8

Twisting Scripture

There is nothing more frustrating than discussing Scripture with Jehovah's Witnesses. They don't care what the Bible actually says. They make it say whatever they want it to say.

Take communion, for example.

Isaac invited me to the Jehovah's Witness annual communion service (it is open to the public). They call it "the Lord's evening meal." It is always an evening service that occurs on the "exact" date that Jesus ate the last supper with his disciples. I decided to go, expecting to see a normal communion service, but nothing could have prepared me for what I saw.

Something odd happened when they passed around the bread. Everyone just passed it around. Nobody partook, except for one person who was sitting right behind me. The same thing happened with the wine. This intrigued me. I ended up having a conversation with Isaac and some other Witnesses after the service. The conversation lasted until midnight.

This is paraphrased, but they told me that only 144,000 persons will be in heaven. These people are born again; some have passed away and some are living today. Only the "born again" partake in communion, and they apparently know who they are. The rest of the Witnesses do not partake in communion because they are not part of the 144,000. They won't go to heaven but they will live happily on the new earth.

By the end of the conversation I was thoroughly confused. We looked at Scripture (John chapter 3 and some verses in Revelation) but I could not see where they were coming from. They were saying one thing and Scripture was saying another. It was not a matter of trying to interpret confusing verses. They were plainly twisting what Scripture plainly says.

As entertaining as that communion service was, I'm going to side with Scripture.

Christians do the same thing

Christians play the same games. They ignore what the Bible clearly says. They twist Scripture, make things up, and grab random verses out of context to "support" their views.

Søren Kierkegaard said, "The matter is quite simple. The Bible is very easy to understand. But we Christians are a bunch of scheming swindlers. We pretend to be unable to understand it because we know very well that the minute we understand we are obliged to act accordingly."[30]

Holy kiss

"Greet all the brethren with a holy kiss" (I Thessalonians 5:26).

"Greet one another with a kiss of love" (I Peter 5:14).[31]

"And when he (Paul) had said these things, he knelt down and prayed with them all. Then they all wept freely, and fell

---

30 Søren Kierkegaard, *Provocations: Spiritual Writings of Søren Kierkegaard*, 2002, Plough, p. 201.
31 See also Romans 16:16; I Corinthians 16:20; II Corinthians 13:12.

on Paul's neck and kissed him, sorrowing most of all for the words which he spoke, that they would see his face no more. And they accompanied him to the ship" (Acts 20:36-38).

Most Christians unashamedly disobey these verses. They claim the holy kiss was a "cultural thing." That is a lie. The holy kiss is a Scriptural commandment.

Christians should not pick and choose what they want to obey and practice from the Bible. *Christians should believe the whole Bible and submit to whatever the New Testament says.*

Head covering

"But I want you to know that the head of every man is Christ, the head of woman *is* man, and the head of Christ *is* God. Every man praying or prophesying, having *his* head covered, dishonors his head. But every woman who prays or prophesies with *her* head uncovered dishonors her head, for that is one and the same as if her head were shaved. For if a woman is not covered, let her also be shorn. But if it is shameful for a woman to be shorn or shaved, let her be covered. For a man indeed ought not to cover *his* head, since he is the image and glory of God; but woman is the glory of man. For man is not from woman,

Up until the mid-1800s, practically all Christian women wore a head covering because of I Corinthians 11:3-10.

but woman from man. Nor was man created for the woman, but woman for the man. For this reason the woman ought to have *a symbol of* authority on *her* head, because of the angels" (I Corinthians 11:3-10).

Women are to cover their heads when they pray or prophesy, and men are to uncover their heads when they pray or prophesy. Paul's instruction and reasoning is very clear, but how many women wear head coverings today? I think the Plain churches are the only ones. I am not condemning women who don't wear a head covering, but they are disobeying God's word.

Women pastors

"And I do not permit a woman to teach or have authority over a man, but to be in silence. For Adam was formed first, then Eve" (I Timothy 2:12-13).

"A bishop then must be blameless, the **husband** of one wife…" (I Timothy 3:2).

It has become very popular for women to become pastors and church leaders. However, God says this job is for men.

Foot washing

"So when He had washed their feet, taken His garments, and sat down again, He said to them, 'Do you know what I have done to you? You call Me Teacher and Lord, and you say well, for *so* I am. If I then, *your* Lord and Teacher, have washed your feet, you also ought to wash one another's feet. For I have given you an example, that you should do as I have done to you. Most assuredly, I say to you, a servant is not greater than his master; nor is he who is sent greater than he who sent him'" (John 13:12-16).

Have you ever washed somebody's feet? Even though Jesus exemplified it (and commanded it), many Christians totally brush it off. In fact, some churches teach against it, claiming it was just a cultural custom of the time in the Middle East.

Raising hands

"I desire therefore that the men pray everywhere, lifting up holy hands, without wrath and doubting" (I Timothy 2:8).

This is clear instruction for men to raise their hands while they pray. Paul didn't specify if he was talking about public or private prayer, but it was probably both. For some reason, many churches frown on raising hands and actually discourage their members from obeying this verse.

Swearing and honesty

"Again you have heard that it was said to those of old, 'You shall not swear falsely, but shall perform your oaths to the Lord.' But I say to you, do not swear at all: neither by heaven, for it is God's throne; nor by the earth, for it is His footstool; nor by Jerusalem, for it is the city of the great King. Nor shall you swear by your head, because you cannot make one hair white or black. But let your 'Yes' be 'Yes,' and your 'No,' 'No.' For whatever is more than these is from the evil one" (Matthew 5:33-37).

"But above all, my brethren, do not swear, either by heaven or by earth or with any other oath. But let your 'Yes' be 'Yes,' and your 'No,' 'No,' lest you fall into judgment" (James 5:12).

Swearing was done in the Old Testament, but was forbidden by Jesus. He said, "Do not swear at all." Therefore, Christians are not to swear. Yet, many Christians ignore these verses and find all kinds of ways to justify themselves.

A true Christian is also totally honest, and he keeps his word. His "Yes" means "Yes" and his "No" means "No."

Separation from the world

"Do not love the world or the things in the world. If anyone loves the world, the love of the Father is not in him" (I John 2:15).

"Adulterers and adulteresses! Do you not know that friendship with the world is enmity with God? Whoever therefore wants to be a friend of the world makes himself an enemy of God" (James 4:4).

In America, there is (sadly) no difference between the Christians and non-Christians. Christians are to be separate! I could mention many examples, but I will only bring up two: sports and entertainment.

When Christianity was young, there was a clear distinction between the Christians and the non-Christians in this area.

Tertullian (160-230 A.D.) said, "We renounce all your spectacles . . . among us nothing is ever said, seen or heard that has anything in common with the madness of the circus,[32] the immodesty of the theater, the atrocities of the arena, or the useless exercise of the wrestling ground."[33]

Novatian (d. 257 A.D.) said, "Idolatry . . . is the mother of all the public amusements."[34]

The early church was passionately on fire for Christ. They were so busy expanding God's kingdom, and being persecuted, they didn't care about who had the fastest chariot or the best stage act.

---

[32] The circus was a race track – not a clown show.
[33] David W. Bercot, ed., *A Dictionary of Early Christian Beliefs*, 2006, Hendrickson Publishers, pp. 231-232.
[34] *Ibid.*, p. 233.

Divorce & remarriage

"And the two shall become one flesh, so then they are no longer two, but one flesh. Therefore what God has joined together, let not man separate" (Mark 10:8-9).

"I say to you that whoever divorces his wife for any reason except sexual immorality causes her to commit adultery; and whoever marries a woman who is divorced commits adultery" (Matthew 5:32).

There are broken homes and broken hearts all over America because of divorce. The church desperately needs to obey these verses and be an example to the rest of the world. God designed marriage for a man and a woman to be joined together for life. Divorce is not an option! And divorce and remarriage is adultery.

When my father was growing up (in the 1950s & 60s), divorce was very uncommon. He went to a public school and remembers only one child in his class from a broken home. Today, it is almost the other way around. It is "normal" for children to be raised in a broken home. God help us.

War & self defense

"You have heard that it was said, 'An eye for an eye and a tooth for a tooth.' But I tell you not to resist an evil person. But whoever slaps you on your right cheek, turn the other to him also. If anyone wants to sue you and take away your tunic, let him have *your* cloak also. And whoever compels you to go one mile, go with him two. Give to him who asks you, and from him who wants to borrow from you do not turn away" (Matthew 5:38-42).

"You have heard that it was said, 'You shall love your neighbor and hate your enemy.' But I say to you, love your enemies, bless those who curse you, do good to those who hate you, and pray for those who spitefully use you and persecute you, that you may be sons of your Father in heaven" (Matthew 5:43-45).

"Repay no one evil for evil" (Romans 12:17).

"Blessed *are* the peacemakers, for they shall be called sons of God" (Matthew 5:9).

Nothing has caused more shame and confusion to Christianity than "Christian war." The New Testament is clear on this subject; yet, so many Christians justify war and self-defense. They would not hesitate to fight and kill other people to defend their selves, country, possessions, or families.

Followers of Jesus are harmless. They are not wimps, but they are filled with the love of Christ. Therefore, they would rather suffer than harm their fellow man. Jesus said the most important commandments are to love God and love your neighbor as yourself (Matthew 22:37-40). And He said "your neighbor" is **everybody** (Luke 10:29-37).

Remember what happened the night Jesus was arrested? Peter used violence to defend Him and cut off Malchus' ear with a sword. Jesus rebuked Peter and healed Malchus' ear (Matthew 26:51-52; Mark 14:47; Luke 22:50-51; John 18:10-11). A few years later (after he was filled with the Holy Spirit), Peter said, "For to this you were called, because Christ also suffered for us, leaving us an example, that you should follow His steps: Who committed no sin, nor was deceit found in His mouth; who, when He was reviled, did not revile in return; when He suffered, He did not threaten, but committed Himself to Him who judges righteously; who Himself bore our sins in His own body on the tree, that we, having died to sins, might live for righteousness – by whose stripes you were healed" (I Peter 2:21-24).

Jesus said, "Behold, I send you out as sheep in the midst of wolves. Therefore be wise as serpents and harmless as doves" (Matthew 10:16).

Holiness

"Be holy, for I am holy" (I Peter 1:16).

"He who sins is of the devil, for the devil has sinned from the beginning. For this purpose the Son of God was manifested, that He might destroy the works of the devil. Whoever has been born of God does not sin, for His seed remains in him; and he cannot sin, because he has been born of God" (I John 3:8-9).

"Keep back thy servant also from presumptuous *sins*; let them not have dominion over me: then shall I be upright, and I shall be innocent from the great transgression" (Psalm 19:13 KJV).

"Pursue peace with all people, and holiness, without which no one will see the Lord" (Hebrews 12:14).

"…He who is in you is greater than he who is in the world" (I John 4:4).

"Will you steal, murder, commit adultery, swear falsely, burn incense to Baal, and walk after other gods whom you do not know, and then come and stand before Me in this house which is called by My name, and say, 'We are delivered to do all these abominations'?" (Jeremiah 7:9-10).

Many Christians claim to be "saved," but continue to sin. They don't think it is necessary to live a holy life. They may avoid sins like drunkenness, stealing, and murder; but they have no problem with sins like impatience, anger, gossip, lust, pornography, hatred, evil thoughts, bitterness, selfishness, complaining, worrying, greed, covetousness, gluttony, fornication, etc.

Christ came to liberate us from sin! If somebody continually lives in unrepentant sin, they have not been saved. A disciple of Christ does not live in sin. They may sin on occasion, but it is followed by repentance. Clement of Alexandria (150-215 A.D.) said, "To be subjected to our lusts, and to yield to them, is the most extreme form of slavery. To keep those lusts in subjection is the only liberty."[35]

The Old Testament Jews fought in physical battles. Similarly, New Testament Christians fight in a daily battle against Satan, sin, and temptation! Paul said, "Fight the good fight of faith" (I Timothy 6:12). He said, "Finally, my brethren, be strong in the Lord and in the power of His might. Put on the whole armor of God, that you may be able to stand against the wiles of the devil. For we do not wrestle against flesh and blood, but against principalities, against powers, against the rulers of the darkness of this age, against spiritual *hosts* of wickedness in the heavenly *places*" (Ephesians 6:10-12).

Modesty

The New Testament instructs women to, "adorn themselves in modest apparel, with propriety (decency) and moderation, not with braided hair or gold or pearls or costly clothing" (I Timothy 2:9).

America idolizes sexual immorality. Movies, TV shows, commercials, billboards, books, and magazines are all saturated with it. Our culture encourages women to flaunt themselves and men to lust. The way girls dress is sad. Tight clothes, barely any clothes, short shorts, miniskirts, low tops, etc. . . . and it keeps getting worse.

Christians should be drastically different from this sex-craved, immoral culture.

Jesus said, "You have heard that it was said to those of old, 'You shall not commit adultery.' But I say to you that whoever looks at a woman to lust for her has already committed adultery with her in his heart" (Matthew 5:27-28). I think every church would say "amen" to this verse. It is sinful for a man to lust after a woman. However, few churches

---

35 *Ibid.*, p. 547.

look at the flip side. It is equally sinful for the woman if she dressed in a way that tempts a man to lust. Christian women should shudder at the possibility of wearing something that might cause men to sin. They should put serious thought into the clothes they wear, perhaps asking themselves, "Would I dress this way to meet Jesus?"

Church leaders have a Biblical responsibility to teach the importance of wearing modest clothes that reflect Jesus Christ. Parents have the responsibility of teaching their children.

Excommunication

"...if your brother sins against you, go and tell him his fault between you and him alone. If he hears you, you have gained your brother. But if he will not hear, take with you one or two more, that 'by the mouth of two or three witnesses every word may be established.' And if he refuses to hear them, tell it to the church. But if he refuses even to hear the church, let him be to you like a heathen and a tax collector" (Matthew 18:15-17).

Does anybody do this?

Obeying government authorities

"Therefore submit yourselves to every ordinance of man for the Lord's sake, whether to the king as supreme, or to governors" (I Peter 2:13-14).

"Let every soul be subject to the governing authorities. For there is no authority except from God, and the authorities that exist are appointed by God. Therefore whoever resists the authority resists the ordinance of God, and those who resist will bring judgment on themselves. . . . Render therefore to all their due: taxes to whom taxes *are due*, customs to whom customs, fear to whom fear, honor to whom honor" (Romans 13:1-2, 7).

"Honor the king" (I Peter 2:17).

Christians are to submit to their governing authorities and respect them. Yet, how often do you hear Christians make comments, jokes, and negative remarks towards authority figures they don't agree with. Obviously, we won't agree with everything the government does, but we are to honor them, love them, and pray for them. The emperor of Paul's day (Nero) persecuted Christians! Did Paul bash him? No. He wrote, "Remind [your church] to be subject to rulers and authorities, to obey, to be ready for every good work, to speak evil of no one, to be peaceable, gentle, showing all humility to all men" (Titus 3:1-2).

The only time Christians should disobey the government is if the government outlaws Christianity or asks them to do something that would violate the teachings of Christ. Then the Christian is forced to "obey God rather than men" (Acts 5:29). Many Christians have suffered martyrdom and/or persecution for being Christians. Some have suffered for obeying Christ. For example, in times of war, many governments have tried to make Christians fight; and persecuted them when they refused.

Bow your heart to the plain words of Scripture

Before beginning a book about hell, Francis Chan said:

> I've spent many hours fasting and praying that God would prevent my desires from twisting Scripture to gratify my personal preferences. And I encourage you to do the same. Don't believe something just because you want to, and don't embrace an

idea just because you've always believed it. Believe what is Biblical.[36]

I will never forget the phrase I heard a minister use one time. He was visiting from another state and was preaching at a local church. My wife and I went to hear him. He preached about the husband and wife relationship and touched on some subjects that people don't like to hear about (responsibility and submission). After he read some verses in Ephesians, he paused and said, "I know this may not be popular, but I need to bow my heart to the plain words of Scripture."

Christians need to bow their hearts to the plain words of Scripture.

At the end of the Sermon on the Mount, Jesus said, "Not everyone who says to Me 'Lord, Lord,' shall enter the kingdom of heaven, but **he who does** the will of My Father in heaven. Many will say to Me in that day, 'Lord, Lord, have we not prophesied in Your name, cast out demons in Your name, and done many wonders in Your name?' And then I will declare to them, 'I never knew you; depart from Me, you who practice lawlessness!' Therefore whoever hears these sayings of Mine, and does them, I will liken him to a wise man who built his house on the rock: and the rain descended, the floods came, and the winds blew and beat on that house; and it did not fall, for it was founded on the rock. But everyone who hears these sayings of Mine, and does not do them, will be like a foolish man who built his house on the sand: and the rain descended, the floods came, and the winds blew and beat on that house; and it fell. And great was its fall" (Matthew 7:21-27).

Justin Martyr said, "Let it be understood that those who are not living by Christ's teachings are not Christians at all

---

36 Francis Chan and Preston Sprinkle, *Erasing Hell,* 2011, David C. Cook, p. 15.

54   *Magnify the Lord*

Through the Creation Museum, many people have been educated on the book of Genesis, learning the truth about dinosaurs, the origin of humans, and the myth of evolution.

– even though they might profess His teachings with their lips."[37]

Answers in Genesis

There is an organization in Kentucky called Answers in Genesis (AiG) that takes a steadfast stand on the first book of the Bible. In 2007, their museum, called The Creation Museum, was opened to the public. Through this museum, many people have been educated about the book of Genesis. They learn the truth about dinosaurs, the origin of humans, and the myth of evolution. AiG (and the Creation Museum) is blessing Christians daily all over the world. Conversely

---
37 David W. Bercot, ed., *A Dictionary of Early Christian Beliefs*, 2006, Hendrickson Publishers, p. 128.

they are constantly being slandered and ridiculed by people who oppose God's word.

Ken Ham (the CEO of AiG) says:

> The reason for much of the conflict throughout the church at the present time is that people are fighting over their opinions. It is not a matter of opinion, yours or mine. It is what God says that matters. The basis for our thinking should be the principles from His Word. . . . One major difficulty in our churches is that many people do not trust Genesis.[38]

I am thankful for the ministry of Answers in Genesis. I'm actually amazed at how much attention they have received, positive and negative, just because they take a stand on one book of the Bible. What if they would take a stand on the whole Bible? That would turn America upside down!

Leading others astray

I was eating breakfast with another Christian one morning and we were discussing the subject of war. We looked at the Sermon on the Mount and discussed what Jesus meant when He said, "Love your enemies." I said, "I believe Jesus really wants us to love our enemies." He said, "That's what Jesus said, but we don't have to actually do it. My pastor explained to me what Jesus really meant."

What Jesus really meant?

Ponder this illustration. Let's pretend there is a man named "Bob." Let's say that Bob treats his wife terribly. He says mean things to her and gets angry at her. He even cheats on her. Bob would be sinning against God, right?

---

38 Ken Ham, *The Lie: Evolution*, 2006, Master Books, p. 69.

Now, what if Bob justifies his behavior and convinces his friends? He tells them God doesn't mind if they say nasty things about their wives and look at other girls. He twists Ephesians 5:25 ("Husbands, love your wives") and says, "Paul didn't really mean for husbands to actually love their wives."

Thanks to Bob, all the men in his neighborhood start denigrating their wives, looking at trashy magazines, and committing adultery. Suddenly, a lot of people are sinning against God.

We do so much damage when we twist the Bible.

In the next two chapters, we will look at two major areas where the Witnesses (and Christians) continue to lead others astray.

Chapter 9

Pride

Jesus spoke this parable to some who trusted in themselves that they were righteous, and despised others:

> Two men went up to the temple to pray, one a Pharisee and the other a tax collector. The Pharisee stood and prayed thus with himself, 'God, I thank You that I am not like other men – extortioners, unjust, adulterers, or even this tax collector. I fast twice a week; I give tithes of all that I possess.' And the tax collector, standing afar off, would not so much as raise his eyes to heaven, but beat his breast, saying, 'God, be merciful to me a sinner!' I tell you, this man went down to his house justified rather than the other; for everyone who exalts himself will be humbled, and he who humbles himself will be exalted (Luke 18:9-14).

Which one of these men reminds you of Jehovah's Witnesses—the Pharisee or the tax collector?

Christians do the same thing

Humility is defined as, "The state or quality of being humble; freedom from pride and arrogance; lowliness of mind; a modest estimate of one's own worth; a sense of one's own unworthiness through imperfection and sinfulness; self-abasement; a deep sense of one's own unworthiness in the sight of God" (Webster's 1828 Dictionary). Scripture says, "For [God] will save the humble people" (Psalm 18:27). "God resists the proud, but gives grace to the humble" (Proverbs 3:34; James 4:6; I Peter 5:5).

Pride is defined as, "The quality or state of being proud; inordinate self-esteem; an unreasonable conceit of one's own superiority in talents, beauty, wealth, rank, etc., which manifests itself in lofty airs, distance, reserve, and often in contempt of others." God says, "Pride and arrogance . . . I hate" (Proverbs 8:13). C.S. Lewis said, "As long as you are proud you cannot know God."[39] Andrew Murray said, "Pride must die in you, or nothing of heaven can live in you."[40]

Followers of Jesus are humble. Yet, so many Christians are proud. Somehow, they think God will let pride into heaven (even though it got Satan kicked out). Some are openly proud. Others find clever ways to disguise it.

Rightness versus righteousness

Some Christians always have to be right. They enjoy arguing. They never admit they are wrong. They run people over. They love to share their knowledge. To them, Christianity is about being right. These Christians may actually be right, but they are proud.

Scripture says, "Let nothing be done through selfish ambition or conceit, but in lowliness of mind let each esteem others better than himself. Let each of you look out not only for his own interests, but also for the interests of others. Let this mind be in you which was also in Christ Jesus, who,

---
[39] C. S. Lewis, *Mere Christianity*.
[40] Andrew Murray, *Humility & Absolute Surrender*, 2005, Hendrickson Publishers, p. 58.

being in the form of God, did not consider it something to be held onto to be equal with God, but made Himself of no reputation, taking the form of a bondservant, and coming in the likeness of men. And being found in appearance as a man, He humbled Himself and became obedient to the point of death, even the death of the cross" (Philippians 2:3-8).

Followers of Jesus shouldn't flaunt their knowledge, put others down, or make sarcastic remarks. They love others more than they love themselves. They admit when they are wrong. Their goal is not to win a debate. Their desire is to help others come to the truth.

I once witnessed an interesting discussion. Two Christians from different denominations were chatting about an issue they did not see eye to eye on. After a while, one Christian decided to cordially end the debate because it was going nowhere. He said, "Joe, I want you to know that I love you." It was one of the most powerful things I ever saw. Unfortunately, the love was not mutual. Joe blew it off and wanted to keep arguing.

Stubborn versus steadfast

I used to work on a hog farm. Moving the hogs from one location to another was always an adventure. The hogs would usually cooperate with a little encouragement but it seemed like there were always some hogs that would give us a headache. They would squeal, resist, and refuse to go where they were supposed to go. These hogs usually ended up killing themselves; they would die from all the stress.

Christians can be just as stubborn as those hogs. They won't budge from their cemented opinions. They squeal, resist, and refuse to listen to the truth. They are stuck in their ways.

Steadfast Christians are different. They don't push their personal opinions or agendas. They humbly submit to truth. They are kind, open, and respectful to others; but they would rather die than disobey God.

This may help you understand the difference:

Stubbornness comes from a human spirit.
Steadfastness comes from the Holy Spirit.

Stubbornness arises from the influence of people.
Steadfastness arises from the influence of the Bible.

Stubbornness is based on opinions.
Steadfastness is based on conviction.

Somebody once said, "Men hold opinions, but convictions hold men."

Paul went from stubborn to steadfast. He was a religious Pharisee who zealously and stubbornly persecuted people who didn't see things his way. Until one day he had an encounter with Christ and everything changed. Trembling and astonished, Paul said, "Lord, what do You want me to do" (Acts 9:6)? From then on, he zealously and steadfastly preached Christ. Hallelujah!

Condemnation versus compassion

I heard somebody make an illustration with the board game called Chutes and Ladders. I assume you are familiar with this game. As you know, there is a chute (slide) just before the winning space. Somebody could be a few steps from victory, but if he or she lands on that chute, he or she will slide down to the bottom. In the same way, somebody could be serving Jesus and living a godly life, but if he starts puffing himself up and looking down on others, he will fall down. Jesus said, "Condemn not, and you shall not be condemned" (Luke 6:37).

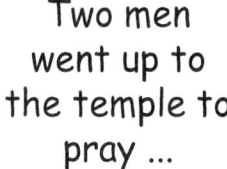
Two men went up to the temple to pray ...

Jesus calls this critical, condemning spirit a "plank in the eye." He says, "And why do you look at the speck in your brother's eye, but do not consider the plank in your own eye? Or how can you say to your brother, 'Let me remove the speck from your eye'; and look, a plank is in your own eye? Hypocrite! First remove the plank from your own eye, and then you will see clearly to remove the speck from your brother's eye" (Matthew 7:3-5). This plank needs to be washed out with tears of compassion.

I remember a time when I was dealing with an obvious sin in my life. A brother came to "help" me and chewed me out. I got upset and defended myself. Later that day, a different brother approached me in love and humbly asked a few questions. There was nothing I could do but acknowledge my sin and hug him for caring about me. I happily repented (and apologized to the first brother).

"Who is wise and understanding among you? Let him show by good conduct that his works are done in the meekness of wisdom. But if you have bitter envy and self-seeking in your hearts, do not boast and lie against the truth. This wisdom does not descend from above, but is earthly, sensual, demonic. For where envy and self-seeking exist, confusion and every evil thing are there. But the wisdom that is from above is first pure, then peaceable, gentle, willing to yield, full of mercy and good fruits, without partiality and without hypocrisy. Now the fruit of righteousness is sown in peace by those who make peace" (James 3:13-18).

Pride versus humility

Pride cares about self.
Humility cares about others.

Pride wants self to be glorified.
Humility wants God glorified.

Pride talks about people.
Humility talks to people.

Pride rebels against authority.
Humility respects authority.

Pride says, "I am right."
Humility says, "God is right."

Pride defends itself.
Humility is dead to self.

Pride needs to be noticed.
Humility notices needs.

Pride is jealous when others are praised.
Humility rejoices when others are praised.

Pride says, "I," "I," "Me."
Humility says, "I love you," "I'm sorry," "Forgive me."

Pride wipes its feet on others.
Humility washes the feet of others.

Be clothed with humility

Scripture says, "Yes, all of you be submissive to one another, and be clothed with humility, for God resists the proud, but gives grace to the humble" (I Peter 5:5).

> He has shown you, O man, what *is* good; and what does the LORD require of you but to do justly, to love mercy, and to walk humbly with your God? (Micah 6:8).

John M. Brenneman said:

> Now, dear readers, having seen the great difference between the proud and the humble, what will we do? The former God resists, but He gives grace to the latter. Which, then, will we choose? God's grace, or to be resisted by Him? I hope we will choose His grace. Though it is not otherwise to be obtained than by passing through the valley of humiliation, let us not on that account be frightened back; but truly bend and humble ourselves. . . . Remember, Jesus was humble.[41]

Andrew Murray said:

> What a solemn thought, that our love to God will be measured by our everyday intercourse with men and the love it displays; and that our love to God

---

41 John M. Brenneman, *Pride and Humility*, originally published 1867, 2012 (reprint), Sermon on the Mount Publishing & Primitive Christianity Publishers, p. 28.

will be found to be a delusion, except as its truth is proved in standing the test of daily life with our fellow men (I John 4:20). It is even so with our humility. It is easy to think we humble ourselves before God: but humility towards men will be the only sufficient proof that our humility before God is real; that humility has taken up its abode in us, and become our very nature; that we actually, like Christ, have made ourselves of no reputation. When in the presence of God lowliness of heart has become, not a posture we assume for a time, when we think of Him, or pray to Him, but the very spirit of our life, it will manifest itself in all our bearing towards our brethren. The lesson is one of deep import: the only humility that is really ours is not that which we try to show before God in prayer, but that which we carry with us, and carry out, in our ordinary conduct. The insignificances of daily life are the importances and the tests of eternity, because they prove what really is the spirit that possesses us. It is in our most unguarded moments that we really show and see what we are. To know the humble man, to know how the humble man behaves, you must follow him in the common course of daily life.[42]

He also said, "I feel deeply that we have very little conception of what the Church suffers from the lack of this divine humility – the nothingness that makes room for God to prove His power."[43]

---

42   Andrew Murray, *Humility & Absolute Surrender*, 2005, Hendrickson Publishers, pp. 25-26.
43   *Ibid.*, p. 28.

Chapter 10

Wealth

It was getting late, and the Soviet officer had beaten and tortured a Christian named Paulus for many hours. Seeing torture was getting nowhere, he tried to think of a different way to break his will and discourage him. He said, "Paulus, we will take away all you own." Paulus wore a beautiful smile and said, "You will need a long ladder, Captain, for my treasures are stored up in heaven."[44]

Jesus said, "Do not lay up for yourselves treasures on earth, where moth and rust destroy and where thieves break in and steal; but lay up for yourselves treasures in heaven, where neither moth nor rust destroys and where thieves do not break in and steal. For where your treasure is, there your heart will be also" (Matthew 6:19-21).

"It is easier for a camel to go through the eye of a needle than for a rich man to enter the kingdom of God" (Mark 10:25).

"You cannot serve God and mammon (wealth)" (Matthew 6:24).

"Blessed are you poor, for yours is the kingdom of God. . . . but woe to you who are rich" (Luke 6:20, 24).

---

44 The Voice of the Martyrs, *Extreme Devotion*, 2001, Thomas Nelson, p. 15.

Materialism, wealth, and the Jehovah's Witnesses

In the book of Acts, Peter and John came upon a lame man. Peter said, "Silver and gold I do not have, but what I do have I give you: In the name of Jesus Christ of Nazareth, rise up and walk" (Acts 3). "And he took him by the right hand and lifted *him* up, and immediately his feet and ankle bones received strength."

Peter and John said, "Silver and gold I do not have." Jehovah's Witnesses say, "Silver and gold I have."

The Witnesses I spoke with came to my house in flashy cars and wore expensive clothes. The men were decked out in fancy suits, brand new sunglasses, twenty dollar haircuts, and a lot of cologne. The women wore stylish clothes and costly jewelry.

You won't need a long ladder to take all they own. Clearly, their treasures are here on earth.

Christians do the same thing

Jesus told a parable about a sower who went out to plant seeds. He said, "Some seeds fell by the wayside; and the birds came and devoured them. Some fell on stony places, where they did not have much earth; and they immediately sprang up because they had no depth of earth. But when the sun was up they were scorched, and because they had no root they withered away. And some fell among thorns, and the thorns sprang up and choked them. But others fell on good ground and yielded a crop: some a hundredfold, some sixty, some thirty" (Matthew 13:4-8).

Jesus explained, "Now he who received seed among the thorns is he who hears the word, and the cares of this world and the deceitfulness of riches choke the word, and he becomes unfruitful."

Does that sound like American Christianity?

David Platt asks a good question: "Is materialism a blind spot in American Christianity today?" He says,

> Surely, this is something we must uncover, for if our lives do not reflect radical compassion for the poor, there is reason to question just how effective we will be in declaring the glory of Christ to the ends of the earth. More pointedly, if our lives do not reflect radical compassion for the poor, there is reason to wonder if Christ is really in us at all.[45]

"Our World and Our Wealth"

There is a gifted teacher from Pennsylvania named John D. Martin who magnifies Jesus all over the country. He boldly preaches on the subject of wealth.

Martin says:

The story is told of a shipwrecked sailor who landed on a South Seas island and was seized by the natives. They hoisted him to their shoulders, set him on a wooden throne, and said that he was going to be king for one year. This man discovered that they did this every year.

But after the man had been king for a little while, he began to wonder what they had done with the previous kings because it appeared that no former kings were living on the island. He was told that after the one-year reign, the king was put on a desert island and left there to starve.

But this man was wise. He hired people to go out to the desert island and fertilize it, build irrigation systems, plant trees, and construct buildings. For the rest of the

---
45   David Platt, *Radical,* 2010, Multnomah Books, p. 111.

year, the king had men working to furnish the desert island with everything a man would need to live there.

Thus, at the end of his reign, the man was banished to an island of plenty, furnished for abundant living.

Now, we all are kings for a little while on this earth. It is our responsibility to decide what we are going to do with the things God has given us. We can keep them here and when we leave have nothing on the other side, or we can send them on ahead to enjoy them for all eternity. That is what the Scripture has clearly said to us. Jesus said, "Lay up for yourselves treasures in heaven."

Then he told us how to do it. He said, "Sell that ye have, and give alms; provide yourselves bags which wax not old, a treasure in the heavens that faileth not." We live in a world that offers us tremendous opportunity to do this with extravagance because we live in a very, very needy world. There is no end to the needs to which we can give.

The reality

Seven billion people live in our world. Are you aware that one billion out of those seven billion live on less than one dollar a day? Another two billion of the seven billion live on less than two dollars a day. In other words, nearly half of the people in our world struggle to find enough food and water just to survive another day. Almost half . . . that is an incredible fact!

Here are some more facts. Every day, 29,000 children die of starvation and preventable disease, brought on by contaminated water, infections, malaria, and the like—29,000 children! To help you think a little bit about that reality, by the time this talk is finished, about 1,000 children in the world will have died from preventable causes. All they needed was food, clean water, or proper medical attention.

Teen Mania, a youth ministry, puts on a yearly event to challenge young people. One year they decided to do a demonstration that would make the realities of the world a little more real. To every session (held in various parts of the country), they brought a gold fish in a bowl. They took the gold fish out of the bowl and laid it on the podium, then stepped back to see what would happen. The audience was left to watch the gold fish flop around and die. In *every* case, someone in the audience could not stand to watch this and ran up to put the fish back in the bowl. The problem is that *you* are not there when those 29,000 children die in obscurity, often in places that the news media does not reach.

Someone once said, "A single death is a tragedy; a million deaths is a statistic." My goal is that by the time you finish reading this article, each one of those 29,000 deaths will be a tragedy, not just a statistic.

The golden rule

Suppose *you* were starving and you knew that some rich teenager could have saved your life if she hadn't needed that sixth pair of shoes. What would you think if you heard that she was a Christian and you knew what Christianity taught? And you died, knowing that this person had the means to save your life but simply did not care . . . what would you think?

Every night, 850,000 children go to bed hungry. How much money would it take to prevent this mind-boggling tragedy in our world? Actually, $13 billion would provide the basic nutrition for every starving child in the world.

You may say, "That is a lot of money!" But are you aware that American Christians spend $21 billion a year on soft drinks? If every Christian in the United States gave the money he or she spent on soft drinks, every starving child in the world would have a full stomach.

Do you want to know how much those same people spend on Christmas gifts? An unbelievable $100 billion! That same money would feed and educate almost every needy child in our world. For $3 billion a year, 500,000 people could be saved from blindness that occurs simply from the lack of vitamin A. American Christians spend $5 billion on bottled water.

But the most heart-wrenching thing going on in our world is an injustice that happens to people who have no choice. In our world, 246 million children are in the bonds of child labor.

All over the third-world countries, destitute people get into financial trouble, perhaps a funeral or an illness that they cannot afford to pay for. Not having the money to put food on the table, their children are sold to bonded-labor men. They may earn 10 cents a day, and the interest gets way ahead of the amount they owe. They will work for years to pay off $10 or $15 that was borrowed. To me, that is heart-wrenching. In fact, it is so heart-wrenching that I must do something about it . . . so much so that I have been talking about it with

my family. I can't handle the fact that 7-year-old children are forced to work like that. What were you doing when you were seven years old?

I want you to think about this. I want to lay a burden on your heart. We live in a country that is unrealistically the richest country that the world has ever seen. I see teenagers in my own community buying designer clothes, buying $160 sneakers, buying soft drinks, buying fancy cars, buying expensive cool clothes, buying 20 pairs of shoes. You know what goes on, even in our Plain communities.

What does God think about all of this?

God has repeatedly admonished and warned us about our responsibilities. Dozens of Scriptures speak about this. We are going to look at some of them. I hope to cure you forever of selfish materialism. My purpose is to show that your indulgence is someone else's suffering. Indulgence cannot be practiced with impunity. It costs someone else for you to be selfish with the resources you have.

Old Testament admonishments

Proverbs 24:11-12 reads this way, "If thou forbear to deliver them that are drawn unto death [and I have just given you some of those accounts] and those that are ready to be slain; If thou sayest, Behold, we knew it not." Now that may have been true years ago, without all the electronic media we have today. But basically nobody today in our society can say, "We don't know that these injustices are happening." It is on your cell phone and computer, even in the newspapers. It is just there, in front of you if you *want* to know it. And the Scripture says, "Don't you say to the Lord, 'We don't know it.'"

The verse continues: "Doth not he that pondereth the heart consider it? and he that keepeth thy soul, doth not he know it? and shall not he render to every man according to his works?" So, don't say "I didn't know it; they were statistics. I didn't actually see it happening." Don't say that! Not a single person reading this can say, "I don't know it; I am going to buy my 20th pair of shoes . . . " Or purchase my dream car. Or build my dream house. Or continue in some other indulgence.

In Proverbs 28:27 we read, "He that giveth unto the poor shall not lack." That is a promise. God said that, not me! Continuing on, we read, "But he that hideth his eyes shall have many a curse." I really don't know what "have many a curse" means, but I don't want to find it out!

Proverbs 21:13 tells us, "Whoso stoppeth his ears at the cry of the poor, he also shall cry himself, but shall not be heard." Jeremiah 22:16–17 states: "He judged the cause of the poor and needy; then it was well with him: was not this to know me? saith the LORD." He is saying that to judge the cause of the poor and needy is to know God. Will God say you knew Him if you ignore the poor to have your luxuries? Continuing on, he writes, "But thine eyes and thine heart are not but for thy covetousness, and for to shed innocent blood, and for oppression, and for violence, to do it."

These are strong Scriptures, and reading them I was much convicted. My life needs some changes, and I intend to make them.

Now let's look at Ezekiel 16:49: "Behold, this was the iniquity of thy sister Sodom . . . " Now if you ask most people what the sin of Sodom was, they would answer, "homosexuality." And that is true. However, God surprisingly says, "Pride, fullness of bread, and abundance of idleness was in her and in her daughters, neither did she strengthen the hand of the poor and needy."

Apparently God puts ignoring the poor in the same category as He puts sexual immorality. God takes our attitude about the poor, as can be seen in the aforementioned Scriptures, very seriously. He has a special eye on the poor; not only for *their* need, but for *your response* to their need. He is watching!

God could deal with all these inequities just like He could save the whole world without missionaries. He could do all of that, but He leaves these situations for His children so that they can accept their responsibilities and do what needs to be done. He is watching my attitude toward the poor just like He is watching my attitude toward the lost. He takes it very seriously!

New Testament admonishments

Let's look at Matthew 25, the classic New Testament Scripture on the subject of caring for the poor. It really doesn't need any comments or explanation.

"When the Son of man shall come in his glory, and all the holy angels with him, then shall he sit upon the throne of his glory: And before him shall be gathered all nations: and he shall separate them one from another, as a shepherd divideth his sheep from the goats: And he shall set the sheep on his right hand, but the goats on the left. Then shall the King say unto them on his right hand, Come, ye blessed of my Father, inherit the kingdom prepared for you from the foundation of the world: For I was an hungred, and ye gave me meat: I was thirsty, and ye gave me drink: I was a stranger, and ye took me in: Naked, and ye clothed me: I was sick, and ye visited me: I was in prison, and ye came unto me. Then shall the righteous answer him, saying, Lord, when saw we thee an hungred, and fed thee? or thirsty, and gave thee drink? When saw we thee a stranger, and took thee in? or naked, and clothed thee? Or when saw we thee sick, or in prison, and came unto thee? And the King shall answer and say unto them, Verily I say unto you, Inasmuch as ye have done it unto one of the least of these my brethren, ye have done it unto me. Then shall he say also unto them on the left hand, Depart from me, ye cursed, into everlasting fire, prepared for the devil and his angels: For I was an hungred, and ye gave me no meat: I was thirsty, and ye gave me no drink: I was a stranger, and ye took me not in: naked, and ye clothed me not: sick, and in prison, and ye visited me not. Then shall they also answer him, saying, Lord, when saw we thee an hungred, or athirst, or a stranger, or naked, or sick, or in prison, and did not minister unto thee? Then shall he answer them, saying, Verily I say unto you, Inasmuch as ye did it not to one of the least of these, ye did it not to me. And these shall go away into everlasting punishment: but the righteous into life eternal."

Most people read this and say, "Well, I thought the final judgment was going to be about whether a person surrendered in obedience unto Christ." That is true. But the response of John the Baptist is interesting when the people came to him—after he had preached that scorching sermon calling them vipers—saying, "What shall we do?"

John responded, "If you have two coats, give one away. If you have more food then you need, give the extra away." What strange advice! You would have expected him to say, "You need to turn from your sins!" Well, he *was* saying that in very practical terms. He was telling them what the fruit of repentance looked like in real life.

If you asked most people what the "fruit of repentance" is, you would get a different picture than what John shared. John told the people that "fruit of repentance" is distributing one's extra material goods. If so, can most Christians say they actually have ever repented?

Zacchaeus came to Christ saying that he was going to give half of his goods to the poor and restore that which he had wrongfully taken. Do you remember what Jesus said to him? "Today is salvation come to this house!" If genuine repentance is giving away your extra stuff, and if salvation is proved by what you *do* with your extra stuff, I ask myself, "How much salvation are we really experiencing?"

In Matthew 25 Jesus makes it very clear what judgment is going to be based on. The evidence that you have surrendered your life in faith and obedience to Christ will manifest itself specifically in how you handle your material goods. According to John the Baptist, Zacchaeus, and what Jesus says in this chapter, there has not been genuine repentance, nor faith in Christ, nor a surrender to His lordship, nor obedience to His commands if we are not sharing with the poor. The thing that troubles me is that for years the church has failed to emphasize this fact of the gospel.

Blinded

There is a great blind spot in American Christianity. It is amazing what kind of blind spots Christians can have. Are you aware that in this country 150 years ago Christians defended slavery? We look back and say, "How in the world could they possibly have defended slavery?" But they did! And *you* can be that blind. I hope that we can rid ourselves of blindness about how God requires us to handle the possessions He lends to us.

The world has 143,000,000 orphans because of all the wars and other social catastrophes. There is an anti-Christian Website that plays the song "Jesus Loves Me" while showing pictures of the emaciated children. Then at the end they show a cross covered by a circle with a line through it that means "No." Then the Website says the following: "He is your God; these are His rules; and you all go to hell." Now granted, that is a pretty awful message, and they don't intend for it to do any good. But I am afraid they understand the gospel better sometimes than we do.

The widow gave all that she had. She gave her living, which literally means she had nothing left for the next day. And Jesus said that she had given more than all the rest put together. That is Jesus' standard: not how much you give, but how much you have left.

I hear people say, "This man is really rich, but he really gives." According to the parable, God does not measure how much you give; He measures *what it costs you* to give.

The requirement is that God expects us to know what is going on in our world and to respond to those needs to the extent of our ability. And He *will* hold us accountable.

The resources

The United States is the richest nation in the world. It has one half of the world's wealth . . . and 5% of the world's population. Did you get that?

In the United States, 160 million adults claim to be Christians. Now think about it: if each professing Christian gave $15 a month, it would literally wipe out starvation in the world. Now I understand that a lot of

Wealth 77

 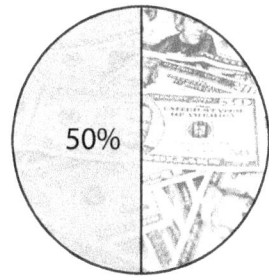

The United States of America has 5% of the world's population ... and 50% of the world's wealth.

the starvation situations are political conditions that make it impossible to even get aid to the needy. We are talking only in hypothetical figures here. Not only would starvation be eradicated, it would supply safe drinking water for all children and educate every child not in school.

God has given us more than what we need for only one reason. Did you know that? 2 Corinthians 8:14-15 gives us that reason: "For I mean not that other men be eased, and ye burdened: But by an equality, that now at this time your abundance may be a supply for their want, that their abundance also may be a supply for your want: that there may be equality."

If you have more than enough to meet your needs, there is only one reason: so you can help those who do not have enough. It is *not* yours to use as you wish. In fact, are you aware that the great practical theme of the Scriptures is equity?

The prophets warned Israel time after time concerning inequity, which means that you respond with your resources in a way that is not equitable, or equal. Instead of equality, you lavish your resources on yourself while there are other people in the world who are dying.

And God hates it! So He has told us through Paul that the reason some people have more than enough is so that they can give to those who have less, and things can equal out.

Getting ahead?

We have a brother in our community who farms organically. He feeds his cattle very little grain—he says it is too expensive—and has basically his whole farm in alfalfa and grazes his cows, without raising any corn. He makes a decent living. He says, "My cows don't get sick. They have little mastitis and no twisted stomachs. My cows stay in the herd for many years, instead of 2 or 3 years like the cows on farms where they are pushed with energy." He was thus telling me what a wonderful experience he has farming. He has healthy cows, and he makes a good living.

I was telling a friend of mine about that and he said, "Yeah, you can make a living doing that, but you can't get ahead."

I said, "What do you mean by 'getting ahead?'"

He replied, "You will never come up with enough money to buy the next farm."

You see, that is our mentality ... "get ahead." My question is, "Get ahead of whom? God?" God said that if you have extra money, it is not yours to do with as you please. It has been given to you because there are people here in the world who need it, and for some reason God has given it to American Christians, expecting it to flow from America to other parts of the world so that there can be at least some semblance of equality worldwide.

We have an unbelievable opportunity. Let's consider the response by looking at 2 Corinthians 9:6 (I love this verse!): "But this I say, He which soweth sparingly shall reap also sparingly; and he which soweth bountifully shall reap also bountifully." This is in the context of giving. Next we read, "Every man according as he purposeth in his heart, so let him give; not grudgingly, or of necessity: for God loveth a cheerful giver."

Do you know what the Greek word for "cheerful" is? "Hilaros!" from which we get our English word "hilarious." God loves a hilarious giver! I mean when he gives, he is in hilarity! It is the most uplifting thing he can think of to do!

God loves such a giver!

Continuing on to verse 8, we read (this verse is taken out of context many times. If you are not living as I was just describing, then this verse does not apply to you): "And God is able to make all grace abound toward you; that ye, always having all sufficiency in all things, may abound to every good work." This is for the hilarious giver. I think we all want that kind of blessing. God has clearly told us how to have it.

In Philippians 4:19 we find another promise: "But my God shall supply all your need according to his riches in glory by Christ Jesus." Again this is in the context of giving. Paul is commending the people in Philippi for sending an offering. Let's look at the verse 17: "Not because I desire a gift: but I desire fruit that may abound to your account." Paul tells them that he is happy to receive the gift, not because it was sent to him but because he knew that the result would be a blessing on their account.

Looking again at verse 19, we see the words "according to his riches." Now if God gives us "according to his riches," that is a little bit different from Him giving "out of his riches." Let me explain . . .

If I were a millionaire, and you had a $50,000 hospital bill and I paid $40,000 of it, you would say that was a pretty good gift. But the amount would give you no clue how wealthy I really am. However if I paid the whole $50,000 bill and gave you $20,000 on top of that, you would have some idea of how wealthy I am. To the hilarious giver, God gives according to His riches—commensurate with His wealth—not "out of his riches." This is a tremendous promise!

The gospel is full of teachings and warnings about materialism, yet everybody wrings their hands in our Plain churches and says, "We are drowning in our materialism . . . " while refusing to obey the Gospel's plain solution to the problem.

Look! We are in a war against the world, and the world is basically a materialistic world that values only the things you can see and feel and touch. The best way to win the war against materialism is by extravagant giving.

Matthew 6:1–4 shows us how our giving is to be done: "Take heed that ye do not your alms before men, to be seen of them: otherwise ye have no reward of your Father which is in heaven."

To the Jewish mind, the word "alms" meant any righteous deed, but we think of it in terms of giving.

"Therefore when thou doest thine alms, do not sound a trumpet before thee, as the hypocrites do in the synagogues and in the streets, that they may have glory of men. Verily I say unto you, They have their reward. But when thou doest alms, let not thy left hand know what thy right hand doeth: That thine alms may be in secret . . . " And here is the part that excites me! " . . . and thy Father which seeth in secret himself shall reward thee openly."

In reaction to the Roman Catholics, with their "means of grace," we have gone to the other extreme and said there are no means of grace. But there are means of grace. One of them is given to us in these verses. When we give alms, God rewards us openly, although not necessarily with money, in return.

Openly rewarded

Let me give you an example of a man whom God rewarded openly in a tremendous way. You probably did not know what was behind the scenes. I am referring to John Wesley.

John Wesley chose to live on what today would be a salary of about $20,000/year here in the United States. He never changed that through his entire life. The hidden side of this is that John Wesley wrote many books and was involved in handling large sums of money, earning approximately $160,000 a year in our economy. Yet he never took out for his own expenses more than the $20,000 salary he paid himself.

I visited the Wesley museum in London where he preached and I stood there convicted. Here was a man who was famous and could have had basically anything he wanted in material goods. He had supporters who would have gladly given him any honor or position he wanted. But John Wesley was a man who cared about the poor in London.

Exhibit after exhibit in that museum show the lengths to which he would go just to help one prisoner or poor person who was in trouble. John Wesley was an extravagant giver. In fact, at one point in his life tea became expensive, and he quit drinking tea so that he would have that much more to give to the poor. He was involved in prison ministry, poor houses, the cause of freeing slaves in England. Basically anybody in need captured John Wesley's heart.

There is a reason that at his death someone made the following comment about Wesley. "When Wesley departed from this world, he left a battered hat, a worn coat, a tattered Bible, and the Methodist Church."

And that was not just a happenstance. His extravagant, self-sacrificing giving explains why God blessed his ministry extravagantly.

Sacrificial love testifieth loudly

Tertullian identified the outpouring of sacrificial love as the key factor to explain the multitudes that came to Christ in those first centuries. Albert Einstein said, "The world is a dangerous place. Not because of those who do evil, but because of those who look on and do nothing." We are to overcome evil with good.

Ghandi was once asked by E. Stanley Jones—who had desperately tried to get Ghandi to make a commitment to Christ—what hindered him from committing his life to Jesus. Ghandi replied, "The Christians."

Suppose we repented of our materialism and became known for our sacrificial and extravagant generosity in obedience to Christ? Yes, some of this does happen, but the people around us also know that we have piles of money left. We are known for our wealth and being people who have money. Suppose we were known as people who have depleted our resources for the sake of God's Kingdom and are the most generous people on the face of the earth . . . Coupled with nonresistance, obeying Christ in hilarious giving would be the most powerful testimony in the world.[46]

---

46   John D. Martin, "Our World and Our Wealth," *The Heartbeat of the Remnant*, November/December 2012, pp. 18-26. Ephrata Christian Fellowship, 400

Tithing and stewardship

Many Christians justify their wealth because they tithe. They give ten percent and keep the rest. Nowhere in the New Testament is that taught by Jesus or His Apostles. Tithing is from the Old Testament.

Some claim that Christians are supposed to be "good stewards of their money," using this phrase as an excuse for investing their money so as to accumulate more wealth. This is also not taught in the New Testament. Christians are instructed to be good stewards of the Christian faith (not money). For example, Jesus tells a sobering parable in Matthew 25. This parable, which uses money as an illustration, explains what happens to Christians who are fruitful ("Well done, good and faithful servant") and Christians who are unfruitful ("Cast the unprofitable servant into the outer darkness"). Paul said, "Let a man so consider us, as servants of Christ and stewards of the mysteries of God. Moreover it is required in stewards that one be found faithful" (I Corinthians 4:1-2).

We should be good stewards of the money which God has given us by doing with it what He has said to do – take care of the needs (not necessarily wants) of ourselves and families, and then give the rest wisely away – giving priority to those who "are of the household of faith" (Galatians 6:10).

In Luke 16, Jesus explains that money is a test. John D. Martin says:

> Let's turn now to some very often misunderstood verses in Luke 16. "And he said also unto his disciples, There was a certain rich man, which had a steward; and the same was accused unto him that he had wasted his goods. And he called him, and said unto him, How is it that I hear this of thee? give an account of thy stewardship; for thou

mayest be no longer steward. Then the steward said within himself, What shall I do? for my lord taketh away from me the stewardship: I cannot dig; to beg I am ashamed. I am resolved what to do, that, when I am put out of the stewardship, they may receive me into their houses. So he called every one of his lord's debtors unto him, and said unto the first, How much owest thou unto my lord? And he said, An hundred measures of oil. And he said unto him, Take thy bill, and sit down quickly, and write fifty." He was still giving away, unjustly, his lord's money!

"Then said he to another, And how much owest thou? And he said, An hundred measures of wheat. And he said unto him, Take thy bill, and write fourscore."

He had no authorization to do this! But he was getting prepared for getting fired.

"And the lord [whom he had just ripped off!] commended the unjust steward, because he had done wisely: for the children of this world are in their generation wiser than the children of light."

This man knew that it was to his advantage to make friends with his lord's money. But we don't understand that. Our Lord says, "Do it!" But we don't do it.

"And I say unto you, Make to yourselves friends of the mammon of unrighteousness; that, when ye fail, they may receive you into everlasting habitations."

Now I don't understand what all that means, but it is clear that we are to do with our money what the unjust steward did with his money. The next part is what I really want to look at.

"He that is faithful in that which is least is faithful also in much: and he that is unjust in the least is unjust also in much." Jesus then explains what He is referring to:

"If ye have not been faithful in the unrighteous mammon, who will commit to your trust the true riches?"

What true riches? The kind that John Wesley experienced. God says, "Money is a test. Money is the least on my scale of importance, and I am going to watch you and see what you do with it. And then when I see what you have done with your money, I will decide whether to give you the true riches, the kind that John Wesley enjoyed in his ministry."

Does that explain why there is so little power, so little gifting, so little effect of our witness and testimony? It may just be that the Lord is looking at the materialism—that we all know exists among us—and the waste of our resources on extravagances, luxuries, and frivolous things, and that He is telling Himself, "If that is what they do with what I consider as the least important thing, I will never give them the things that are really important."

Let's turn now to Isaiah 58:10-11 and consider some tremendous promises, given in the context of fasting. "And if thou draw out thy soul to the hungry, and satisfy the afflicted soul; then shall thy light rise in obscurity." John Wesley didn't live in obscurity. Everybody knew who he was. I am not saying we should seek for fame, but that is what the Bible says.

"And thy darkness be as the noonday. And the LORD shall guide thee continually, and satisfy thy soul in drought, and make fat thy bones: and thou shalt be like a watered garden, and like a spring of water, whose waters fail not." This is a promise given to those who reach out their hand to the poor.

Christians do practice this principle to a degree, and what they do proves that these promises are true. After Hurricane Katrina, Christians sacrificed to give the city food, water, and shoulders to cry on. It was obvious to the people of New Orleans that the Christians were doing the lion's share of the restoration work. A Jewish doctor looking on made this comment after it was over: "There are no longer any agnostics in New Orleans."[47]

Church inequity

Jesus said, "A new commandment I give to you, that you love one another; as I have loved you, that you also love one another. By this all will know that you are My disciples, if you have love for one another" (John 13:34-35).

Before leaving this subject, I want to address something that puzzles me. I see Christians struggling financially who are forced to turn to the government for aid. Meanwhile, sitting beside them at church are wealthy Christians with money piled up. That is not right.

Christians should take care of each other. Scripture says, "Now the multitude of those who believed were of one heart and one soul; neither did anyone say that any of the things he possessed was his own, but they had all things in common. And with great power the apostles gave witness to the resurrection of the Lord Jesus. And great grace was upon them all. Nor was there anyone among them who lacked; for all who were possessors of lands or houses sold them, and brought the proceeds of the things that were sold, and laid *them* at the apostles' feet; and they distributed to each as anyone had need" (Acts 4:32-35).

There was no caste system in the early church. It was a loving brotherhood. They made sure that nobody lacked, and distributed to each as anyone had need. What an excellent model! Obviously, Christians should not be freeloaders – I am not encouraging anybody to be lazy – but the church should take care of its members who need financial assistance. Then together, they can help everyone around them.

Sadly, the government and insurance companies have taken the place of the church.

---
[47] *Ibid.*, pp. 24-25.

Suits & retirement

I want to throw out a few more challenges. Why do Christians wear expensive clothes to church? For example, most men wear suits. Where did this idea come from? Christians should wear the same clothes to church that they wear every other day – clothes that are inexpensive and modest. Something is wrong when poor people aren't coming to church because they don't own a suit. Christians should not make poor people feel uncomfortable. Christians should make rich people feel uncomfortable.

What about retirement? Gary Miller shares:

> In the minds of (most) people, retirement is a non-negotiable right and relaxation a goal worth striving for – in spite of the fact that many retirees spend day after meaningless day vegetating and wistfully longing for some diversion.
>
> But is this what God has in mind? Does He intend for healthy men and women to coast out of life without vision or purpose? The Bible is clear that God has a much higher vision, and we have many examples like Moses, Abraham, and the Apostles who served God until the end. Whatever your age, God has something for you to be involved in.[48]

Give

> *"Gold is tested by fire, and man is tested by gold."*
> *–Chinese Proverb*

"There was a certain rich man who was clothed in purple and fine linen and fared sumptuously every day. But there was a certain beggar named Lazarus, full of sores, who was laid at his gate, desiring to be fed with the crumbs which fell from

---
48   Gary Miller, *Going Till You're Gone*, 2012, TGS International, p. 108.

the rich man's table. Moreover the dogs came and licked his sores. So it was that the beggar died, and was carried by the angels to Abraham's bosom. The rich man also died and was buried. And being in torments in Hades, he lifted up his eyes and saw Abraham afar off, and Lazarus in his bosom. Then he cried and said, 'Father Abraham, have mercy on me, and send Lazarus that he may dip the tip of his finger in water and cool my tongue; for I am tormented in this flame.' But Abraham said, 'Son, remember that in your lifetime you received your good things, and likewise Lazarus evil things; but now he is comforted and you are tormented'" (Luke 16:19-25).

Paul said, "But godliness with contentment is great gain. For we brought nothing into *this* world, *and it is* certain we can carry nothing out. And having food and raiment let us be therewith content. But they that will be rich fall into temptation and a snare, and *into* many foolish and hurtful lusts, which drown men in destruction and perdition. For the love of money is the root of all evil: which while some coveted after, they have erred from the faith, and pierced themselves through with many sorrows" (I Timothy 6:6-10 KJV).

John D. Martin said:

> Will we be remembered as the generation that rose up for the cause of world poverty the best we could with our small numbers? Or will our history show that we were the most selfish generation in history who loved its soft drinks, fancy cars, cosmetics, extravagant clothes, expensive electronic gadgets, oversized houses, and costly vacations?[49]

---

49 John D. Martin, "Our World and Our Wealth," *The Heartbeat of the Remnant*, November/December 2012, p. 26.

Chapter 11

Dishonesty with History

One thing that really gives Jehovah's Witnesses a bad name is their refusal to be honest with history.

False prophesies

When I found out that Jehovah's Witnesses made numerous false prophesies, I asked Isaac about it. He vehemently denied it.

Trinity

Witnesses totally ignore the historic position of the church on the Trinity.

The cross

Witnesses say, "Jesus Christ did not die on a cross." They claim, "the cross had nothing to do with Jesus Christ. The cross is, in fact, pagan in origin."[50]

That is make-believe. All historical evidence reveals that Jesus died on a cross. The Old Testament even alludes to the cross. Justin Martyr (100-165) points out, "Moses himself

---

50 Watch Tower Bible and Tract Society of Pennsylvania, *What Does the Bible Really Teach?*, 2009, Watchtower Bible and Tract Society of New York, pp. 204-205.

prayed to God, stretching out both hands, and Hur with Aaron supported them during the whole day . . . For if he gave up any part of this sign, which was an imitation of the cross, the people were beaten."[51]

Christians can get carried away with the cross: jewelry, tattoos, etc. That is probably what turns the Witnesses off (although it is no excuse for them to make up lies). Mark Minucius Felix (2nd or 3rd century) said, "We neither worship nor wish for crosses."[52]

Christians do the same thing

American Jesus

This is not a big deal, but it is a good example of how Christians ignore history. Most pictures of Jesus published in the United States make Him look like an American. We don't know what Jesus looked like (and it really doesn't matter), but we do know that He looked like the average Jew of His day. He did not look like an American, and He did not have long hair.

Head covering

Most Christians ignore the history of the head covering. Only a few churches practice it today, but for almost two millennia, every church practiced it.

Warren Henderson said:

> The practice of women covering themselves with a veil has been an accepted spiritual exercise throughout the history of the church. Scholars, teachers, and church leaders from the dawning days of the

---
51 David W. Bercot, ed., *A Dictionary of Early Christian Beliefs*, 2006, Hendrickson Publishers, p. 184.
52 *Ibid.*

Dishonesty with History

church age to present have explained passionately its biblical relevance and spiritual significance. Presently, only a few groups of Christians still practice this symbolic display of divine order. Will it be possible for Christendom to resurrect this visible symbol of God's order in the church during the 21st century?[53]

Hippolytus (c. 170-236 A.D.) wrote:

> Let all the women have their head covered with an opaque cloth, not with a veil of thin linen, for this is not a true covering.[54]

"Perfect" heroes

The Bible tells history like it was. However, that is not how most Christians treat history. Usually, Christians only look at the good side of their historical heroes. If their hero had a fault, they excuse it or ignore it completely. Case in point, Christians who lift up the theology of Martin Luther and John Calvin ignore the fact that they persecuted other Christians and were responsible for their deaths.

Martin Luther (c. 1483-1546). Christians who lift up the theology of Martin Luther and John Calvin ignore the fact that they persecuted other Christians.

---

53 Warren Henderson, *Glories Seen & Unseen*, 2007, Warren Henderson, p. 34.
54 From Hippolytus's work *The Apostolic Tradition*; translation quoted from David Bercot, "What the Early Christians Believed About the Head Covering," CD from Scroll Publishing Co.

Christians also ignore the historical faults of their churches.

War

The early Christians did not go to war. I want to be sensitive to Christians who have lost loved ones in a war. At the same time, we have to be historically honest.

Here are just a few quotes that represent how all the early Christians felt about war:

Justin Martyr (c. 100-165 A.D.) said, "We who formerly murdered one another now refrain from making war even upon our enemies."[55]

Lactantius (250-325 A.D.) said, "How can a man be just who hates, who despoils, who puts to death? Yet, those who strive to be serviceable to their country do all these things . . . When they speak of the 'duties' relating to warfare, their speech pertains neither to justice nor to true virtue."[56]

Tertullian (160-230 A.D.) said, "Our religion commands us to love even our enemies, and to pray for those who persecute us."[57]

It wasn't until a Roman Emperor named Constantine embraced Christianity in the fourth century that the church as a whole compromised and started fighting. Thus, Christians have been shedding blood "in the name of Jesus" from the fourth century to the present. Meanwhile, the first three centuries of Christianity are ignored.

---

55 David W. Bercot, ed., *A Dictionary of Early Christian Beliefs*, 2006, Hendrickson Publishers, p. 676.
56 *Ibid.*, p. 680.
57 *Ibid.*, p. 678.

Revolutionary War

It breaks my heart when Christians join the patriotic bandwagon and glorify war (the American Revolution). These Christians claim the American colonists had justifiable reasons for rebelling against their government. They lift up the revolutionists and regard them as glorious Christians.

This couldn't be further from the truth. The American colonists had no Scriptural reasons to disobey their government, and Christians should never *rebel* against their government. Furthermore, the revolutionists were definitely not Christ-like examples. I am not just sharing my opinion. I am comparing their lives to the teachings of Jesus. The revolutionists butchered Indians, murdered Loyalists, enslaved blacks, killed their enemies, and persecuted peaceful Christians (like the Amish, Quakers, Moravians, and Mennonites). I humbly ask, is that what Jesus would do?[58]

I'm thankful to live in America. But I am ashamed of its history.

The revolutionists butchered Indians, murdered Loyalists, enslaved blacks, killed their enemies, and persecuted peaceful Christians.

---

58 I highly recommend the book *In God We Don't Trust*, by David Bercot, available from Sermon on the Mount Publishing.

Mormons do the same thing, too!

The Church of Jesus Christ of Latter-day Saints (Mormons) call themselves Christians, but they put all their focus on a man named Joseph Smith Jr. (1805-1844). The Mormons think Smith was a godly prophet who gave us the Book of Mormon and died a martyr's death.

Joseph Smith Jr. (1805-1844)

In 1844, Joseph Smith Jr., his brother Hyrum, Willard Richards, and John Taylor were arrested for inciting a riot. These four Mormons were placed in the Carthage Jail (which was more like a house) in Illinois. On the afternoon of June 27, they were visited by Cyrus Wheelock, who smuggled in a gun. Smith gladly received it. That night, an armed mob stormed the jail to kill the Mormons. They fired some shots and Smith fired back. Joseph and Hyrum Smith were both killed in the shootout.

In 2012, I met with two Mormon missionaries. They showed me a video the Mormon Church created about the life of Joseph Smith Jr. The video displayed Smith to be a holy prophet of God. It was pretty convincing. At the end of the video, Smith was "innocently" sent to the Carthage jail like a "lamb to the slaughter." When the armed mob came,

Dishonesty with History

Artist's impression of the interior of the Carthage Jail during the murder of Joseph Smith.
"Didn't Joseph Smith have a gun?"

he didn't fight back. He died peacefully. The movie ended with him ascending up into heaven.

Here was our conversation after the video:

> ME: Wow. That was a pretty amazing video. If it's true, then I'll become a Mormon.
> MORMON 1: It was 100% true.
> MORMON 2: Matt, I testify to you that the Mormon Church is right and Joseph Smith is a prophet.
> ME: Are you guys sure that video was true? I mean, did it fabricate some things or leave some things out?
> MORMON 1: It was 100% true.
> MORMON 2: Matt, as sure as the sun is in the sky, the movie was completely true.
> *Slight pause*
> ME: Didn't Joseph Smith have a gun?
> *Awkward silence*

MORMON 2: (*Looking down at the ground*) Yes Matt . . . there was a gun.
MORMON 1: There was?!

Historical integrity

Christians need to look at history with an open, unbiased heart. Too many Christians embrace their doctrines, beliefs and opinions, and ignore history if they don't like what it says.

I recently read an article by Mike Atnip. He is an Anabaptist author and amateur historian. His article addresses the ordination of women, but his main point is historical integrity. He said:

> Integrity has to do with "wholeness." When speaking of a person's or a group's integrity, it carries the idea of being totally honest. For myself, when dealing with Anabaptist history it means admitting—for as much that I admire the Anabaptist movement—that there were some things I cannot agree with. Some of them held wrong ideas about divorce/remarriage. Some of them had really—I mean *really*—funny ideas about eschatology....
>
> So what do you do with a person or a group who does not seem to have integrity with history? Personally, I find it hard to swallow the same person's (or group's) handling of the Holy Scriptures. If they pull an ambiguous quote from Martyrs Mirror and make it appear that the early Anabaptists had ordained women eldresses, or if they use one ambiguous early church quote, but ignore a dozen plain ones . . . how will they handle the Bible? . . .
>
> Does integrity ignore obvious evidence to the contrary? That said, simple, honest ignorance can also be involved. Innocent ignorance does not mean a lack of integrity. The difference is when truth is revealed,

innocent ignorance will acknowledge its former error. A lack of integrity will just make excuses or ignore the truth . . .

One of integrity's mightiest foes is having an agenda. For example, concerning church history, it is common (and I have found myself doing it as well) to go looking in history to find support for a position, instead of to go looking for what position the historical evidence provides. And the same, of course, applies to looking in the Bible to find evidence to support an agenda . . .

Yet, I realize that sometimes when I read—be it the Bible or history—I sense that an agenda lurks in the shadows, trying to get *me* to ignore evidence that may contradict my current understanding of an issue. May God help us all to flee from all agendas except the "agenda" to be honest seekers of truth. If the truth of the matter is that the early church and the Anabaptists did ordain women to be preachers to men, then may we have enough integrity to say so. If not, then may we just have enough integrity to not twist and hide evidence so as to support an agenda.[59]

---

59 Mike Atnip, "The Ordination of Women and Integrity with History," *The Heartbeat of the Remnant*, May/June 2013, pp. 4-9.

Chapter 12

What Can We Learn from Jehovah's Witnesses?

Though they are tainted by a dark cloud of Russellisms, there is one thing about the Witnesses that constantly impresses me. They are a group of people who are working together and walking in the same direction.

Is that the testimony of your church?

Peter Hoover said:

> ... every local church must constantly work at keeping itself in Gospel order. And that order, I believe, will only be as good as the spiritual level of every local church. A level best diagnosed and maintained through daily life together, through constant, frequent communion meetings where we all hold ourselves and one another accountable to the high standard of our Lord Jesus Christ.[60]

Amen!

---

60 Peter Hoover, "Is Uniformity the Answer?," www.scrollpublishing.com (Accessed June 18, 2013).

A church is a brotherhood

This is such an important subject. I wrestled and wrestled with this chapter because I just couldn't find the words to express what I wanted to say. However, a friend of mine gave me an article from Mike Atnip that masterfully articulated what was on my heart.

Mike said:

Tucked away in the middle of the Mosaic Law is, of all things, the following building code:

"When thou buildest a new house, then thou shalt make a battlement for thy roof, that thou bring not blood upon thine house, if any man fall from thence" (Deuteronomy 22:8).

Now we know that the letter of the Law is not meant for the New Testament believer, but we understand that from its principle we can gain an insight into the Kingdom of God. Thus, from the prohibition of plowing with an ox and a donkey—just two verses below our text—Paul could admonish us to not be "unequally yoked together with unbelievers." From another Mosaic precept, he instructs us that "muzzle not the ox that treadeth out the corn" means that we should materially support those who are laboring in the spread of the Gospel.

What can we, the citizens of the Kingdom, learn from a command to "make a battlement for thy roof"?

What is a battlement?

The first thing to settle is the definition of a "battlement." The Hebrew word used for battlement comes from a root word meaning "to repress, or hold back" that is not used in any other place in the Bible. However, the context gives us a clear picture of the intention of a battlement: to keep people from falling off the roof, which in that

If someone fell off his roof because of the lack of a battlement, the owner of the house was responsible for his death.

culture was usually flat, and used for various purposes. So while the English word "battlement" has connotations of a defensive knee wall—such as might be found on top of the walls surrounding a castle or city—the whole gist of our text is simply that of keeping people from accidentally falling off the roof. And the builder of the house was responsible to see that an appropriate wall was built around his housetop. If someone fell off his roof because of the lack of a battlement, the owner of the house was responsible for his death.

What is a battlement not for?

This may seem to be a redundant question, but for the purpose of our study it will profit us to review a few things that a battlement is not intended for. First of all, a battlement is not a prison wall. In other words, the purpose of a battlement is not that of trying to make sure that the people on the roof can in no way, shape, nor form escape from the roof. Second, a battlement is not used to keep people on the street from getting onto the roof. Thirdly, a battlement is not meant to be used as a nice way to have seating all the way around the edges of the roof, nor a nice place to take a nap. Neither are they to be used for children as a place to play "follow the leader" and practice their balancing act. These are rather rudimentary facts, and it seems almost senseless to review them. Yet, as we proceed, we will find that many people are foolishly misusing battlements.

How tall should a battlement be?

Deuteronomy gives us no details on exactly how a battlement should look. God gave humanity common sense, and He expects us to use it sometimes. A three-inch wall simply will not serve to prevent someone from falling over the edge of a roof. In fact, such a ledge may well cause more falls than it stops. On the other hand, an eight-foot wall is unnecessary and will block off the fresh breezes and sunlight, making the rooftop an undesirable place to be.

An ideal height is somewhere in the range of the navel of an adult person. If it is much lower, whoever might happen to trip and fall against the wall will have the mass of his body weight to be higher than the top of the wall. The center of his gravity will be higher than the wall, making him unable to stop himself from going on over. While there is no reason forbidding one from building the wall higher, it is not necessary. Any person falling over a wall that is higher than his bottom rib had to be doing something abnormally foolish. No one has ever accidentally fallen over a wall that was as high as his rib cage.

Building a spiritual battlement

From these few points, we will now move into the spiritual realm and determine what we can learn from this building code. First of all, the "house" that is being built by some man is the church of God. We, as believers, constitute this house, and Jesus is the master builder. But as coworkers with him, we also are involved in the building of the house, so the statute does concern us.

Let's take it one step further. Instead of thinking in terms of the universal church of Christ, let's look at a local congregation. Christ is building it, and we are his colaborers. His plan calls for a battlement, to keep men from accidentally falling off the roof. What does all this mean, in practical terms?

The battlement of the conscience

As men are called into the house to be a partaker of the benefits of its shelter and direction, there needs to be a "safety wall" built around its edges. This is the conscience, which warns men that "here is the edge; any further and you will drop off." For those whose heart and goal is to stay on the roof, this wall is a blessing. Not that they need it every day, but during a lifetime of labors, sooner or later each person will likely make that stupid step backwards, or trip over that child's toy, which would have sent them hurtling to the street. Thankfully, a wall was there to stop them!

As mentioned above, congregational battlements are not intended to be prison walls. If someone's heart is not set on staying in the house, the battlement can seem like so much a nuisance; after all, they reason, are not we mature enough to know better than step off a roof?

But how many times has your conscience saved you in that weak moment? That time of temptation where you would have fallen to the street with a splat, except something hindered you? However, if you are trying to escape from the roof, the battlement is of little use: one hop or a stepstool will get you over with little effort. So it is with the conscience. If you really want to do something that is not allowed "in the house," all you have to do is leap over the wall.

How to build a church conscience

How does a local congregation build a community conscience? Sure, building a personal conscience is easy; just read the Bible and let the Spirit guide you to the precepts that it contains. After a while, you have a personal conscience built up to what you have perceived as being the will of God. Even a family conscience is not that hard, if Dad and Mom and children are living in harmony. Dad takes the lead, Mom follows and supports, and the children respect them and allow Dad and Mom to specify what is good and right for the home. The children's consciences are slowly built up to what Dad and Mom construct in the children. By the time the child is mature, he has a battlement built up within him that will keep him in those mistakes and close calls.

But all too often this same method does not work in local congregations. Why?

Actions and reactions

One of the biggest causes of failure in building a community conscience lies in reacting to others' failures. People misuse battlements, and the next person reacts. For example, instead of using a church conscience to aid in mishaps, some have tried to use battlements as prison walls to fence in folks who obviously have more interest in what is going on in the street than in the activities of the house. Seeing the youth lined up at the wall, leaning over and chattering with the people below, the builders laid a few more blocks on the battlement, making it head high. Then, when the same youth got some stools to stand on so they could see out and continue their communication with the people below, the builders built another layer or two on the battlement.

Did that stop those disinterested in the activities of the house from their activities? No, they simply got out some stepladders. Looking at this whole situation, some have shaken their heads and come to a conclusion: all this battlement building is useless! Determined to do things "the right way," they moved down the street and decided that they were NOT going to use battlements to keep folks penned in. So they built a new house . . . without any battlements.

"Who needs battlements?" they reasoned. "If a man is careful and minds his business, he can stay away from the edge. We just simply need to be mindful and be more faithful to warn each other, and no one will fall over the edge." So they built "virtual" battlements, ever mindful that real battlements do not keep worldly folks in the house from fellowshipping with the world.

This is, of course, a reaction. What needs to happen to those whose heart is not in the activities of the house is that the elders need to gently but firmly take them downstairs and say to them: "It is obvious that your heart is on the street. Here you are, go. When your heart is changed, we welcome you back." Hard decision, I know, but that is what the father of the prodigal son did. It was best for both of them.

Virtual battlements

Many years ago, I worked on a construction job in the State of Wyoming that required safety inspections by OSHA standards. One of the specifications was that any scaffolding over so many feet off the ground (I forget the details) had to have a safety railing around it. Now most construction workers look at OSHA rules like a lot of people look at the Bible: a list of rules that they try to see how much they can get away with, instead of how much they can better put into practice.

Since the inspector did show up about every day, we complied to the rules, at least outwardly. One incident stands out in my mind. We had built a scaffold about 20 feet high, but had not gotten around to putting the railing on yet. Suddenly, someone noticed that the inspector had showed up, and I was instructed to quickly build a railing for the scaffold. With a couple of 2X4s and some wire, I hurriedly tied on some uprights for posts, and with another long 2X4 I made a rail, tied on with a piece of wire. The inspector eventually made his way up to where I was working, and stood there looking over the situation.

As I was on good terms with him, I laughingly said something like "Look, we have a railing. Just don't lean on it; it might fall off!"

I expected a shake of the head and possibly a reproof with orders to build a real railing. To my great surprise, he just quietly answered, "That's fine. All that railing is needed for is a warning to someone who backs up into it that he is near the edge. It doesn't need to be able to stop someone from falling."

I felt relieved and happy to hear that on that day. But there is another side to the story.

Had I tripped over something on the scaffold that day and hit that "virtual railing," it would not have saved me from a trip to the pavement 20 feet below. Had that misfortune occurred, my opinion of "virtual railings" would have probably bottomed out.

The big question

This brings us to an important question for builders of battlements: Does a "virtual battlement" meet the requirements of Deuteronomy 22:8? Does a 2X4 tied loosely on a wobbly stake provide enough protection against falling off a roof, so that whoever trips over the edge is guilty of his own blood? For a temporary construction situation as I told about, a virtual railing is acceptable, perhaps even necessary, since the workers have to constantly be reaching out of the scaffold to do their work. But for a housetop, virtual railings do not work.

Let's look at a real historical example. About a century before Martin Luther came along, a revival of primitive Christianity occurred in Bohemia. Fashioning their lives according to the Sermon on the Mount, these brothers built communities of believers throughout the land. Whoever desired to be a part of these churches had to agree to align his life to the teaching of Jesus, and to live that out in practical ways. Not every aspect of life was spelled out, but the brotherhood had come up with some practical applications—a battlement to surround them—that a person had to agree to before he could join. One example was to not engage in dice-making. Dice were used primarily for gambling, and the brotherhood did not want to be associated with dice-making.

Time passed and along came Martin Luther. At first, Luther was not impressed with these Bohemian brothers—"sour-looking hypocrites and self-grown saints" he called them. But as time went on, he had a change of mind. He told them later:

"Tell your Brethren to hold fast what God has given them, and never give up their constitution and discipline. Let them take no heed of revilements. The world will behave foolishly. If you in Bohemia were to live as we do, what is said of us would be said of you, and if we were to live as you do, what is said of you would be said of us."

"We have never," he added in a later letter to the Brethren, "attained to such a discipline and holy life as is found among you, but in the future we shall make it our aim to attain it."

History tells us that neither Luther nor his churches ever attained it. His virtual battlement was too weak to hold his movement from falling into the street. The lesson? Churches without battlements eventually go over the edge.

The next big question

How does a church build a real battlement? How is a conscience—solid biblical convictions engraved into the heart—built?

Building a battlement consists of solid teaching of biblical principles, backed up by real-life applications to those principles. At the same time, it is made known that there is a line—or in this case a wall—that is not to be crossed on purpose. Whoever willfully climbs over the wall will not be allowed to climb back in, without genuine repentance. In this way, the person on the roof cannot claim that he never realized the danger. When he makes that forgetful step backwards, something will stop him: the teachings and admonishments that he received. When he trips over the toy on the floor, that pure doctrine with practical applications will be as a "battlement" to stop him from going all the way over.

The battle over written standards

Some churches have tried to build a stronger battlement by having a written standard that all members must adhere to. While the example of the Bohemian Brethren may have seemed to be just that, I do not think that all their applications were written out. The bottom line is, one would need a fat, fat book to spell out all the real-life applications to biblical principles.

Let's consider dangers on both sides of the "written standards" issue. There is a danger with written standards, namely that only those applications that are spelled out become the battlement. In other words, suppose that we have 25 applications spelled out on a paper, but the reality is that biblical applications touch hundreds of other areas of our lives. The danger is that one can begin to think that there are no further applications than those that are written down.

Now the reverse: there is a danger in not writing out any applications, namely that people get the idea that the congregation has no expectations. Everyone lives by his own application without regard to others.

I have seen both kinds of shipwreck; it is a toss-up as to which one is more disastrous. Let's look at a real life example of both kinds.

Applications without principle

It is common knowledge that some Mennonite churches have a standard that all cars be black, some even requiring a black bumper. While some may snuff their noses immediately at such a requirement, I am slow to do so, even though I currently drive an all-white minivan.

Back when cars first began to be mass-produced, some of the Mennonites looked at the issue of horseless carriages and decided that there was no inherent spiritual harm in these contraptions, and that it could be consistent with Christian character to use them. Others were not sure about that and stuck to horses. However, those that did decide to use the motorized vehicle decided that if one did get a car, it should be a plain one, not all spiced up with fancy colors or shiny accessories.

Henry Ford had said concerning his product: "The customer can order any color of car he desires, as long as it is black." And so every car that rolled off his new assembly line was black, just like all John Deeres are green. Keeping in line with the biblical principle of simplicity and modesty, the first Mennonites to get vehicles kept them simple: plain ol' black cars.

Time moved on, and as cars began to be more common, some worldly folks wanted to stand out from the crowd and began to want other colors of cars besides plain ol' black ones. Ford Motor Company caught on, and soon one could order other colors. Then came accessories: running lights, reflectors, chromed mirrors and bumpers, and a host of other options. The Mennonites, or at least some of them, kept right on using plain ol' black cars.

More decades passed. Cars kept evolving, and the customer kept demanding more and more options, and car companies kept competing for the market by adding more options. By this time, so many people wanted such a variety of colors, a solid black car was just one option out of maybe 25, and chrome bumpers became standard equipment.

Fast forward to 1985. I am visiting a Mennonite congregation that requires black cars. On my visit to this particular congregation, I learned how the system operated. All of the young men would wash and wax their cars on Saturday evening, preparing them for the Sunday morning lineup, where they were all parked side by side in one gleaming black row. Once while riding with a friend that attended there, I became very puzzled when he turned onto a gravel road and began to drive about 10 mph—something extremely out of place for one who usually was on the other end of the speedometer. At my question as to why, he remarked, "Well, I already washed my car (it was a Saturday afternoon), and I don't want to get it dusty before tomorrow. I am driving slow so I don't stir up dust (and get my car dusty for the lineup tomorrow morning)."

Somewhere along the line, the application lost some of the principle.

Principles without applications

A scene comes to my mind that illustrates the opposite ditch. I was relaxing in my house one Sunday afternoon when a single, young man came to visit us. Knowing him well, I could tell he was disturbed about something. But rather than ask him about it, I thought I would just let it come out naturally. He chatted small talk for a few minutes, then suddenly burst out, "I thought this church didn't have any standards?!"

He was referring to the fact that the congregation did not publish a written standard.

"What do you mean?" I asked.

He spilled out his story. He was from a far western state and was planning to go visit his family. At the same time, he found out an elderly lady in the congregation was planning on visiting the same state. As neither of them had much in material means, immediately the idea clicked in their minds: Why not him ride along with her, help her with the driving, and split the costs? They immediately made plans to leave in a couple of days.

But their plans were squashed by a concerned minister in the congregation. Hearing of their plans, he approached them and said, "I trust both of you, and know you mean well, but I do not think it would be a good testimony for an unmarried man and woman to drive 1500 miles together."

The young man came to my place to let off his steam. "She's old enough to be my grandmother! You can't tell me this church doesn't have a standard!" He was thinking that no written standard meant no congregational applications to real-life, everyday situations; a sad mistake to make.

Rodeo in the church

For a final story, I will relate a true situation, as I was told it. The bishop of a conservative Mennonite church was once questioned why he did not want his church to take the no-written-standard approach for his congregation. "Why, it would be a rodeo!" he exclaimed.

Some ten years later, this same bishop had a change of heart concerning the matter. Following a brothers' meeting, the congregation decided to do away with a written standard. When he was later reminded of

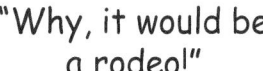
"Why, it would be a rodeo!"

his earlier statement and asked the outcome of that decision, the bishop replied, "Why, we had a rodeo! The very next Sunday all the clothes came out of the back of the closets!"

Let's park here on this incident, and look at it with an objective mind. Which type of administration failed?

Immediately, we see the failure of the no-written-standard approach. The very next Sunday, the people of the congregation "took their liberty" and dressed themselves in clothes that, according to the bishop's words, were not in line with the principles of a converted heart. Their changing from a written standard to an unwritten standard did not help them one iota. But upon a closer look, we also see the failure of the written standard administration. While the worldly clothes did not openly appear, they were there in the back of the closet all the time. In this case, both types of administration failed to deliver the people from their carnality.

The bottom line

The bottom line of this whole matter is that both the "unwritten standard" and the "written standard" administrations have strengths and weaknesses. The reality is that there is no type of church administration that can change a carnal heart, if that heart has decided to love what this earth holds out to him. When the members lose their interest in the business of the house and turn it towards the goings on in the street below, a common response is to just add on another layer of rules, turning what was supposed to be a battlement into prison walls. On the other hand, others want nothing to do with "rules" and so they sigh and breathe a prayer, hoping that things will turn out alright in the end. And so the battlement turns into a yellow warning tape stretched around the perimeter of the rooftop, printed with "We recommend that you do not step beyond this line."

Whose conscience rules?

Does individual conscience trump the community conscience, or does the church conscience overrule each individual's perception of right and wrong? Again, we find extremes on both ends, and plenty of shipwrecks to learn from.

On the rocks of "church conscience only," we find the remains of congregations who are like mindless zombies, able only to quote the 35 rules of the statute book. As to why Statute 25 states that such and such should be done, these folks can only tell you "because that is the way it has always been, and that is what the church says." As far as any personal convictions to shield them from danger while operating outside the sphere of the 35 written rules—which is actually the majority

The ship wrecked because some turned the rudder right while others were turning the sails to make her go left.

of the time—they have none. And so a whole list of inconsistencies stare them in the face; but they are blind to them, since the rulebook has obliterated any personal conscience.

Meanwhile, on the reefs of "individual conscience only" we see the flotsam of congregations who have rejected any community conscience. Many of these ships have hit these reefs by trying to make really, really sure they miss the rocks of "church conscience only." Their only compass was each man's own opinion, and the ship wrecked because some turned the rudder right while others were turning the sails to make her go left.

The community conscience

Any group of people working together has to come to some common agreements. If two carpenters are building a house, one cannot make his walls eight feet tall while the other builds his section seven feet tall. One or the other has to give up his will, or the house will be one big mess.

In the same way, any congregation of believers has to develop a "community conscience." Can a church survive if one member is telling everyone to get involved in politics and the next is telling everyone it is a sin to get involved in it? Will a congregation prosper if some families have a conscience against contemporary music, while other families invite the children over and have them listen to it, telling them there is nothing wrong with it?

A brotherhood has to come to a common consensus on the basics of real-life, practical issues. Whether they then administrate this consensus by "written standards" or "unwritten standards" is somewhat beside the point. As mentioned, both administrations have strengths and weaknesses.

Submitting to my brother's conscience

In 1 Corinthians 10:23-33, Paul gives us a great secret to achieving our goal of unity. The key phrases are "Let no man seek his own, but every man another's *wealth* (well-being)," and "why is my liberty judged of (ruled by) another *man's* conscience?"

An example of being ruled by another's conscience would be the case of the young man I mentioned earlier who was thinking to travel with the older lady. His conscience gave him liberty to do that, but his brother's conscience did not. Whose conscience was to rule? According to Paul, the concerned brother's conscience was to override the young man's "freedom," since his brother did not feel comfortable with the situation. This is called submission, a word our human nature hates with a passion. Needless to say, any congregation that does not practice this type of brotherly submission is headed for a shipwreck.

Romans 14 also deals with this submission. The verse often misused in this chapter is the following: "For the kingdom of God is not meat and drink; but righteousness, and peace, and joy in the Holy Ghost." In a situation where there is a clash of opinions on an issue, this verse often comes up, with one side telling the other: "The kingdom of heaven is not about such issues, so I do not need to listen to you." However, that is exactly the opposite of the meaning of that verse.

Paul is really saying, "Since the kingdom of heaven is not centered on what a person eats or drinks, then why do you fuss when your brother tries to forbid you from eating something? Submit yourself and give it up for his sake! It won't hurt your walk with God to give it up, since the kingdom is not centered on that!"

A final word on the conscience

Before leaving this theme, a warning is necessary. Don't depend entirely on conscience—either community or personal. The conscience is not the final rule of authority in the Christian life. Jesus the Word and the Holy Spirit are the final authorities; the conscience is only a tool in their hands. Some people make the grievous error of letting their—or the community's—conscience be their lord. In fact, such people are idolizing the conscience by making it lord of their life. These folks never grow in their Christian life, and usually end up drifting into more and more worldliness, slowly but surely, since their conscience has no outside input. Let Jesus—not your conscience—be your Lord. Let Him define your battlement, not your battlement define Him.

To depend on the conscience without the lordship of Jesus is like Eutychus in Acts 20, who misused the windowsill. Windowsills are not beds. Neither are battlements. Don't sleep on them!

In conclusion

The conscience—both personal and community—is our battlement, a safety wall in times of weakness and mishap, and a gentle, constant reminder of the line between the roof and the ground below. Used correctly, they are a great blessing. Remove them, and you may someday find yourself lying on the pavement below, one mangled mess.

May we recognize there are "diversities of operations" and be careful in condemning those who don't "operate" exactly like we do. May we act—and not react—when we see others misusing battlements. And finally, may God bless you as you build battlements for your house![61]

---

61   Mike Atnip, "On the Building of Battlements," *The Heartbeat of the Remnant*, March/April 2010.

Chapter 13

What Jehovah's Witnesses Do Right!

A few years ago I was involved in a Bible study that met every Tuesday night for twelve weeks. It was a blessing, but something happened during that study that I will never forget.

The last study was on evangelism. The week prior to that study, somebody suggested that we actually go out and evangelize (instead of just talking about evangelism). The room got quiet for a long time. Finally, somebody sarcastically said, "Yea, and we can pass out Watchtower magazines." Everybody laughed and the subject was dropped.

That made me think – we should not be making fun of the Witnesses for evangelizing. We should be evangelizing!

There are some things the Witnesses do right.

Evangelism

The Witnesses blow us away with their evangelistic zeal. Christians should have the same zeal. Charles Spurgeon said, "Have you no wish for others to be saved? Then you are not saved yourself."[62]

At the same time, it is extremely crucial to point people in the right direction. Jesus said, "Can the blind lead the blind? Will they not both fall into the ditch?" (Luke 6:39).

For example, some Christians want to "save" everyone, so they water down Christianity to make it more appealing to sinners. They don't mention sin, repentance, or discipleship. They don't say anything about the Sermon on the Mount or obedience. They just say something like, "Ask Jesus into your heart so you can go to heaven." This method just brings sinners into the Church.

Jesus said, "Go therefore and **make disciples** of all the nations, baptizing them in the name of the Father and of the Son and of the Holy Spirit. **Teaching them to observe all things that I have commanded you**; and lo, I am with you always, even to the end of the age" (Matthew 28:19-20).

Abortion

"For you yourself produced my kidneys; You kept me screened off in the belly of my mother. I shall laud you because in a fear-inspiring way I am wonderfully made. Your works are wonderful, as my soul is very well aware. My bones were not hidden from you when I was made in secret, when I was woven in the lowest parts of the earth. Your eyes saw even the embryo of me, and in your book all its parts were down in writing" (Psalm 139:13-16; NWT).

While Christians continue to battle over whether or not abortion is acceptable, Jehovah's Witnesses universally teach against it. They say, "according to the Mosaic Law, causing the death of a baby in its mother's womb was wrong.

---

62 Charles Spurgeon, "She Was Not Hid," April 15, 1888, www.spurgeongems.org (Accessed April 11, 2014).

Yes, even such a life is precious to Jehovah (Exodus 21:22-23). This means that abortion is wrong."[63]

Multiculturalism

"There is neither Jew nor Greek, there is neither slave nor free, there is neither male nor female; for you are all one in Christ Jesus" (Galatians 3:28).

"There is neither Greek nor Jew, circumcised nor uncircumcised, barbarian, Scythian, slave nor free, but Christ is all and in all" (Colossians 3:11).

Jesus said, "whoever does the will of My Father in heaven is My brother and sister" (Matthew 12:50). God's family does not consist of one cultural group. There are Christians in North America, South America, Africa, Europe, Asia, and Australia. Scripture says, "For You were slain, and have redeemed us to God by Your blood out of every tribe and tongue and people and nation" (Revelation 5:9).

Few churches understand this as well as the Witnesses. They have churches all around the world. Their fellowship includes individuals from all kinds of different cultures. Sadly, most churches only fellowship within their culture. Even sadder, some Christians are actually racist.

Christians should be the ones teaching against racism. Humans are all related (Acts 17:26). We all descended from Adam and Eve. Minor differences (like color of skin) are insignificant.[64]

---

63 Watch Tower Bible and Tract Society of Pennsylvania, *What Does the Bible Really Teach?,* 2009, Watchtower Bible and Tract Society of New York, p. 127.
64 For more information on racism, go to www.answersingenesis.org.

So many Christians have a tendency to reverence a building.
Perhaps this is why chapels have become so massive, expensive, and attractive.

Simple church buildings

"For you are the temple of the living God. As God has said: 'I will dwell in them and walk among them. I will be their God, and they shall be My people'" (II Corinthians 6:16).

"Do you not know that you are the temple of God and that the Spirit of God dwells in you? If anyone defiles the temple of God, God will destroy him. For the temple of God is holy, which temple you are" (I Corinthians 3:16-17).

God's house is not a particular building. Scripture says, "<u>We</u> are the temple of the living God." It doesn't matter where Christians meet. Some Christians meet in homes. Persecuted Christians meet anywhere they can (barns, fields, wherever). Yet, so many Christians have a tendency to reverence a building. Perhaps this is why churches have become so massive, expensive, and attractive.

Charles Spurgeon said,

> Under the old Mosaic dispensation God had a visible dwelling-place among men. . . . It is a sad fact, however, that there is so much Judaism in all our hearts, that we frequently go back to the old beggarly elements of the law, instead of going forward and seeing in them a type of something spiritual and heavenly, to which we ought to aspire.
>
> It is disgraceful to the present century to hear some men talk as they do. I remember to have heard a sermon once upon this text—"If any man defile the temple of God, him will God destroy." And the first part of the sermon was occupied with a childish anathema against all who should dare to perform any unhallowed act in the churchyard. . . . Can holiness dwell in bricks and mortar? Can there be such a thing as a sanctified steeple? Can it possibly happen that there can be such a thing in the world as a moral window or a godly door post? . . . It is but an extravaganza of an error into which we all of us are likely to fall. We have a reverence for our plain chapels; we feel a kind of comfort when we are sitting down in the place which somehow or other we have got to think must be holy.
>
> Let us get rid once and for ever of all superstitions with regard to place. . . . The house of God is built with the living stones of converted men and women, and the church of God, which Christ hath purchased with his blood—this is the divine edifice, and the structure wherein God dwells even to this day.[65]

---

65 Charles Spurgeon, *The Tabernacle of the Most High*, www.biblebb.com (Accessed July 28, 2013).

We can learn a lot from the Witnesses. They build simple, inexpensive Kingdom Halls. To them, a meetinghouse is just a place where Christians can gather together.

Training children

"And you, Fathers, do not provoke your children to wrath, but bring them up in the training and admonition of the Lord" (Ephesians 6:4).

The following instruction comes from Jehovah's Witnesses:

> Since Jesus took time for little ones, should you not do the same for your own sons and daughters? They need, not small bits of your time, but large amounts of it. You need to take time to teach them, for that is what Jehovah instructs parents to do (Deuteronomy 6:4-9).[66]
>
> On the night before Jesus died, his disciples argued about who was greater among them. Rather than become angry with them, Jesus lovingly continued to appeal to them by word and example. If you are a parent, can you see how you might follow Jesus' example in the way you correct your children? True, they need discipline, but it should be given to "the proper degree" and never in anger. You would not want to speak thoughtlessly "as with the stabs of a sword." (Jeremiah 30:11; Proverbs 12:18) Discipline should be delivered in such a way that your child will later see how appropriate it was.[67]

---

66 Watch Tower Bible and Tract Society of Pennsylvania, *What Does the Bible Really Teach?*, 2009, Watchtower Bible and Tract Society of New York, p. 139.
67 *Ibid.*, p. 141.

One of the chief responsibilities of the Church is to train the next generation. Witnesses seem to understand this. Christians however, are woefully neglecting this responsibility.

Tedd Tripp says:

> We teach (our children) to find their soul's delight in going places and doing things. We attempt to satisfy their lust for excitement. We fill their young lives with distractions from God. We give them material things and take delight in their delight in possessions. Then we hope that somewhere down the line they will see that a life worth living is found only in knowing and serving God. . . . No wonder we lose our kids.[68]

Denny Kenaston said:

> God wants us to raise our children to be a reflection of His glory, and of His work in these last days upon the earth. That is what He is saying to all of us. It is not right that there be just one or two godly homes here and there that get the attention of searching heart(s). . . . There ought to be so many dedicated families in the church that we have many examples to follow. May God work by His Spirit in such a way that the church of Jesus Christ be filled with godly families. The church should be filled with godly fathers and mothers with a zeal, with a vision, and with a vibrant Christianity that they can pass it on to their children. Then those children will take those hot coals and pass them on to their children, and on down the line it will go.[69]

---

68 Tedd Tripp, *Shepherding a Child's Heart*, 2005, Shepherd Press, pp. 45-46.
69 Denny Kenaston, *The Pursuit of Godly Seed*, 2003, Home Fires Publishers, p. 72.

The kingdom of God

"Now after John was put in prison, Jesus came to Galilee, preaching the gospel of the kingdom of God, and saying, 'The time is fulfilled, and the kingdom of God is at hand. Repent, and believe the gospel'" (Mark 1:14-15).

"He (God) has delivered us from the power of darkness and conveyed (translated) us into the kingdom of the Son of His love" (Colossians 1:13).

Jehovah's Witnesses believe in two distinct, separate, opposing kingdoms on this earth. They teach that Christians are part of the kingdom of God while everybody else is part of the kingdom of the world.

We have to be honest. The Witnesses are right on. If you read through the four gospels, you will find "the kingdom of God" was Jesus' main message.

David Bercot, a scholar of early Christianity, said,

> When Christianity was young, Christians recognized the Kingdom of God as the primary authority in their lives. They were first of all citizens of God's Kingdom and only secondary citizens of the earthly nations in which they lived. Their fellow countrymen were all of the other citizens of God's Kingdom around the world. Furthermore, they recognized Jesus as their ultimate Lawgiver and His Sermon on the Mount as their primary Constitution.[70]

What changed? Bercot explains, "in the 4th century, Christians changed their focus from advancing the Kingdom of God to trying to create a 'Christian' world. In the end, they

---

70 David Bercot, *What is a kingdom Christian?*, 2013, Scroll Publishing, CD Jacket.

didn't Christianize the world. Rather, the world sucked them in."[71]

Jehovah's Witnesses line up with historic Christianity. They don't blend God's kingdom with an earthly kingdom. You won't find any Jehovah's Witnesses serving in the military or holding a position in the government (they don't even vote). The Witnesses don't try to impose their beliefs on earthly kingdoms. Their desire is to bring individuals into God's kingdom.

I think that is thrilling! Obviously, the Witnesses don't represent true Christianity, but they understand the concept of the two kingdoms. What if all the Christians in America would see themselves, first and foremost, as citizens of God's kingdom and pledge their total allegiance to Jesus Christ?

---

71 *Ibid.*

Chapter 14

The Gospel of the Kingdom

I want to end with some inspiring words from John D. Martin:

> My concern for this message is to expose a detour that our Anabaptist churches took in the past century. As I was growing up, the message that I heard was what I call a "save ME gospel." Now the term "kingdom of God" was used very loosely—as it is in many church circles—but I don't think I ever heard, in all my growing up years, a message specifically on the kingdom. In this message I want to make it very clear what the kingdom of God is.
>
> It is *not* about us! That is where the problem came in the shift of focus when I was growing up. The main thing in the messages that I heard was "We need to get saved!"
>
> That certainly is true, but "getting saved" is a means to an end; *not* an end in itself. Unfortunately, "getting saved" was made an end in itself, and much of the revival preaching was focused on that end. Therefore, I would like to make it clear what the original gospel of Jesus Christ really was.

> **Kingdom Route Closed**
>
> **Use Individual Avenue**

My concern for this message is to expose a detour that our Anabaptist churches took in the past century.

The original gospel message

The original gospel was the *gospel of the kingdom*. Jesus began His ministry by saying, "Repent . . . " Now, the classic words usually following this would be, " . . . or you will be lost," or "you will go to hell!"

But Jesus did *not* say that. He said, "Repent, for the kingdom of heaven is at hand." In other words, "The kingdom is right there for you to grasp, it's at hand." Six verses later, after calling His first four disciples, it says He "went about all Galilee . . . preaching the gospel of the kingdom." (Mt. 4:23) Do you know that Jesus never called the gospel anything else but "the gospel of the kingdom"? In every instance where you find the content of the gospel described, it is "the gospel of the kingdom." Every time, in the entire gospel record!

Jesus' two most important statements were the Sermon on the Mount and the Lord's Prayer. Both of these begin and end with an emphasis on the kingdom of God. "Blessed are the poor in spirit; for theirs is the kingdom of God." "Thy kingdom come. Thy will be done in earth, as it is in heaven."

Referring to the end of time, Jesus said, "And this gospel of the kingdom shall be preached in all the world for a witness unto all nations; and then shall the end come." I ask you a searching question: Has the gospel of the kingdom been preached unto the ends of the earth, or has it been a "save ME gospel"?

Now I want to make one thing clear before proceeding: God uses imperfect means. I believe the gospel has been preached in many parts of the world, and despite a wrong emphasis, many people have been reconciled to God.

Parables of the kingdom

Basically all of Jesus' parables focus on the kingdom: the kingdom is as a treasure in a field, the kingdom is as a merchant, the kingdom is as a net, the kingdom is as leaven, the kingdom is as a mustard seed.

I want to ask you a question: If I were to ask you what the seed was in the parable of the sower, what would you say?

[Response from someone in the audience: "The Word of God!"]

That's what most people say! And that is true in a general sense, but *specifically* it says it is the "word of *the kingdom*"! I never noticed that until recently. We are so used to reading our Bible through certain lenses. Six months ago I would have probably said the same thing [as the responder from the audience.] When Jesus interprets the parable of the tares, He says the seed is "the children *of the kingdom*." That excites me!

Here I am, speaking to approximately 400 seeds! What should happen is that all you seeds will go out there and be planted and grow up to be a kingdom expression of the gospel! Not just a personal experience of people getting ready to go to heaven, but a kingdom expression of the gospel should grow up around every kingdom Christian. Because you are the "seed of the kingdom."

The kingdom in church history

But, when we turn to the history of the church, it is not very far along before we see a drastic change in focus. How many of you can recite the "Apostles' Creed"? [A few raise hands.] Tell me, what is the word that the Apostles' Creed begins with?

"I."

That's interesting! The Lord's Prayer begins with "Our Father." Neither the Apostles' Creed nor any of those other major creeds after the first centuries say a single thing about the kingdom. Only the Creed of Constantinople says at the end, "… and He shall come again to judge the living and the dead, whose kingdom shall have no end." It places the kingdom "out there" somewhere in the future, but says nothing about its present reality.

The result of losing the kingdom centrality in the gospel is a difference in a person's outlook. If the focus is on ME, then the preaching I heard all my life was truly "gospel preaching," where the most important thing in the world is for me to "get saved." And before I proceed, I want to make it clear that "getting saved" is a very important thing, and heaven and hell are two very important realities we must resolve in the right way.

But that is *not* God's most important concern for the present age. What God wants is a *corporate expression, a society of the redeemed*. Thus, personal salvation is an important *means to an end* and not an end in itself. God cannot express His kingdom until He has redeemed people that He can use to *show to everyone what the whole world would be like if everybody obeyed the King!*

That's what Christianity is all about. We are talking about community, society, corporate relationships, so that the world looking on can say, "Wow!" It is like what the queen of Sheba said when she saw Solomon's court: "What a great God they must have! What a beautiful kingdom! I cannot believe what I see! I did not know that human beings could live together this way!"

That's what kingdom is all about!

But you see, if you concentrate only on your personal salvation and you don't really make the kingdom to be the heart of your gospel—as did Jesus, Paul, and the others who labored to teach it—then you have individual Christians who have no vision for submission to a corporate practice. I wonder just what the world looking on does see?

The great paradigm shift

Now, I stand here guilty with all of you; we have all been involved in this paradigm shift. It is because we have not been taught that *the end of our salvation is to be involved in something larger than ourselves.*

The kingdom of God is the society of the redeemed. As I mentioned, this gospel of the kingdom was lost in the early centuries to an individualistic salvation. And during the last century Anabaptism swallowed it also, and we wonder why we have so much individualism now. It is the fruit of a distorted gospel. We need to get back—it is a burden of my heart—to the kingdom gospel, instead of a "save ME gospel."

Jesus used the word "kingdom" (in reference to the kingdom of heaven or the kingdom of God) at least 124 times, and He never referred to the gospel as anything else. If Jesus focused on the kingdom, then that is the centrality of His message, not a marginal issue. He said, "I must preach the kingdom of God to other cities also: for therefore am I sent." (Lk. 4:43) He tells us very explicitly why He came—to preach the kingdom!

Gospel distortions

Is the kingdom ever taught today? Well, in dispensationalist circles, the kingdom is to happen somewhere off in the future. You know, I think the Devil has used every strategy he can think of to get the focus off the kingdom. I really do! So the dispensationalist has put the kingdom off into the future . . . it is coming. This makes Jesus' teaching irrelevant for today. That is what some people do with the teaching about the kingdom.

Other people, such as Augustine and Calvin, made the kingdom the central theme of their teaching, but it was a carnal kingdom ruled by force. Thus we have these two distortions, two wrong concepts, of the kingdom of God. So the message is lost.

Why did Jesus focus His message on the kingdom of God? Because that was God's original purpose; that is why man was created. Salvation was *not* the main theme of God's original work with man. Man was not "lost" when he was created. God created man so that he would have dominion and express God's authority on this earth.

The first use of the word kingdom in the Bible is in Exodus 19:6, where it states, "And ye shall be unto me a kingdom of priests." That makes it very clear what serving God is all about. We are mediating God's rule on earth. He is the King; we are simply His subjects expressing His rule and authority, first of all in our own lives and fellowships, and then to the conscience of the world around us. Notice God says "ye shall be unto *me*," not unto us (as humans) a kingdom of priests. The purpose of the kingdom is to show God's benevolent rule, through us.

The world does not understand God. When they think about God, they view Him as a negative entity, as some sort of grumpy sovereign out there who enjoys giving lots of rules to make life hard. His ways are not good, and if you follow them, you will never be happy. That is the world's concept of God. Therefore God's purpose is that through this society of the redeemed, this little colony of heaven on earth, the world would get a glimpse of His true attractive character and have a desire to respond properly to Him.

Now the Devil has perverted the idea of the kingdom, which is why people have difficulty with it. Some leaders have perverted the idea of God's kingdom and left a bad taste in our mouth. In the Old Testament, God initially wanted all men to be that kingdom of priests, but this purpose got lost, so He chose a nation. We will not take the time to do so now, but it is an interesting study to go through the Old Testament and see what God wanted to do with that nation. He told them, "I want to lift you up on high, so that all the nations will say, 'What a God they have! What laws they have! What nation has been more blessed?'" He said, "I will make you the lender and not the borrower. You will be number one among the nations . . . *if* you keep all of my commandments."

You see, that is the only way people will be blessed, by a total surrender. Now, I told you of the fragmentation that has taken place in our churches. We don't understand submission of our lives to God and to each other for the sake of the kingdom of God.

> *I want you to forget about yourself, and get your relationship with God established, and then lose yourself in something bigger than yourself!*

The kingdom come!

We saw that in the Old Testament that God wanted a kingdom that would demonstrate to the whole world what a nation would look like if God was the King. And only briefly did the world ever see that, under David and somewhat under Solomon. That was it. Then we come into the New Testament.

I want to show you that the preaching of the gospel as being the *gospel of the kingdom* didn't end with Christ. My goal with this message is to make all of you *passionate church builders*. I want you to forget about yourself, and get your relationship with God established, and then *lose yourself in something bigger than yourself!*

Look in Acts 19:8. What did Paul preach? "And he went into the synagogue, and spake boldly for the space of three months, disputing and persuading **the things concerning the kingdom of God**." The kingdom of God was Paul's message; it was *not* a "save ME gospel." Now look at Acts 20:25. "And now, behold, I know that ye all, among whom **I have gone preaching the kingdom of God**, shall see my face no more."

I want to ask you another searching question. When you "preach the gospel," do you preach the kingdom of God? I hope so, and if you haven't been doing so, I hope you start! Now let's go to the end of Paul's life, described in Acts 28:23. "And when they had appointed him a day, there came many to him into his lodging; to whom he **expounded and testified the kingdom of God**." Again, we see that *the kingdom* was the message! Then after Paul ends up a prisoner in his own rented house, what is he preaching in the very last verse of Acts? "The kingdom of God!"

Now, I think if Paul's gospel had been a "save ME gospel" it would not have been stated that way. The coming of the kingdom of God was the message.

A present reality

This kingdom is a present reality, and the effects of the kingdom show, as in 1 Corinthians 14:23-25. This is what should happen when the kingdom is genuinely expressed.

If therefore the whole church be come together into one place, and all speak with tongues, and there come in those that are unlearned, or unbelievers, will they not say that ye are mad? But if all prophesy, and there come in one that believeth not, or one unlearned, he is convinced of all, he is judged of all: And thus are the secrets of his heart made manifest; and so falling down on his face he will worship God, and report that God is in you of a truth.

This is the kind of authority that the gathered body has when it is gathered in unity. It is a true kingdom expression of authority. Psalm 89:7 tells us that "God is greatly to be feared in the assembly of the saints, and to be had in reverence of all them that are about him."

The ekklesia

What is the church, as denoted by the Greek term *ekklesia*? If you ask most people what that means, they will say, "the called out ones." My question is, "called out to what?" Are they called out just to enjoy each other's fellowship?

In Acts 19, when the uproar took place in Ephesus, the town clerk came on the scene and said, "We are going to be criticized for this disorder. If something needs to be resolved, there is a proper order. If anything needs to be done, it shall be determined in a lawful *ekklesia* (assembly)."

If you had gone to a Greek town and asked for the *ekklesia*, they would have taken you to the town council! It was a governing body; *ekklesia* means a body of people *called out to govern (guide, lead)*. Now suppose you went to the U.S. Congress when they were dismissing, and asked them what had happened that day. Suppose they said, "We had a wonderful fellowship together! We were so encouraged! We had a fellowship meal, and it was a wonderful potluck dinner; you should have seen it! I was so glad I came to Congress, because I was so discouraged, but now I am really inspired!"

You would probably say, "That is not the reason you were supposed to be meeting together! You were *not* supposed to be there for yourself! You were supposed to be there to make good laws for this country, for yourself, for the assembly, and for the whole nation."

A kingdom of peace

And that is why *we* are here, to give guidance to the nations. The early church demonstrated that. Concerning the *Pax Romana* (two hundred years of internal peace in the Roman Empire, with no major wars or disruptions) history books tell you that it was because the Roman army was so formidable and its punishments so terrifying that other nations dared not resist Rome's rule. But if you read the early church writings, you get a different story. They say the reason for those 200 years of peace—which coincided with the first centuries of the church—was that the Prince of Peace had come and established a kingdom of peace, and this kingdom's prayers and influence were keeping the world at peace! Interestingly, those 200 years of peace ended about the same time that the early church began to lose its practice of nonresistance.

The most tragic compromise the church ever made was its compromise of nonresistance.

Since that time, some of the most horrible things have happened "in the name of Jesus": the Crusades, the Inquisition, slavery in America, the American Civil War, and World Wars I and II.

People say, "What do you do with a man like Hitler?" Well, most of the people in Germany were Lutherans. If the church had never lost its stand on nonresistance, Hitler would have had no army! Almost none of the wars in Western civilization would have ever occurred. Do you see now what happened to this kingdom? It got messed up with tragic and unspeakably horrible consequences.

I have to tell you—and I have heard this in testimonies from various people—that the most powerful testimony of the church has been its testimony of nonresistance. We live in a world that is sick of war, hatred, violence, killing, and all the things that go along with war. To hear that there is a group of people—the Anabaptists—who for 500 years has been able to live together in peace without the sword is about the most appealing message we could ever give to the world.

I hope that by now you understand what the gospel of the kingdom is: a gospel that says, "Yes, God wants to save human beings and take them to heaven, but the *most important* part is that He wants them to be an expression of His kingdom here on earth." I will again state my definition of the kingdom of God:

A group of people who

show to everyone

what the whole world would look like

if everybody obeyed the King![72]

---

[72] John D. Martin, "The Gospel of the Kingdom," *The Heartbeat of the Remnant*, September/October 2012, pp. 4-8.

Chapter 15

Come Holy Spirit

Early Anabaptist leader Peter Riedemann said:

> The Church of Christ is the basis and ground of truth, a lantern of righteousness, in which the light of grace is borne and held before the whole world, that its darkness, unbelief and blindness be thereby seen and made light, and that men may also learn to see and know the way of life. Therefore is the Church of Christ in the first place completely filled with the light of Christ as a lantern is illuminated and made bright by the light: that his light might shine through her to others.
>
> And as the lantern of Christ hath been made light, bright and clear, enlightened by the light of the knowledge of God, its brightness and light shineth out into the distance to give light to others still walking in darkness, even as Christ himself hath commanded, 'Let your light shine before men, that they may see your good works, and praise God, the Father in heaven.' Which thing, however, cannot be other than through the strength and working of the Spirit of Christ within us. As, however, the outward light sheddeth a ray and beam, in accordance

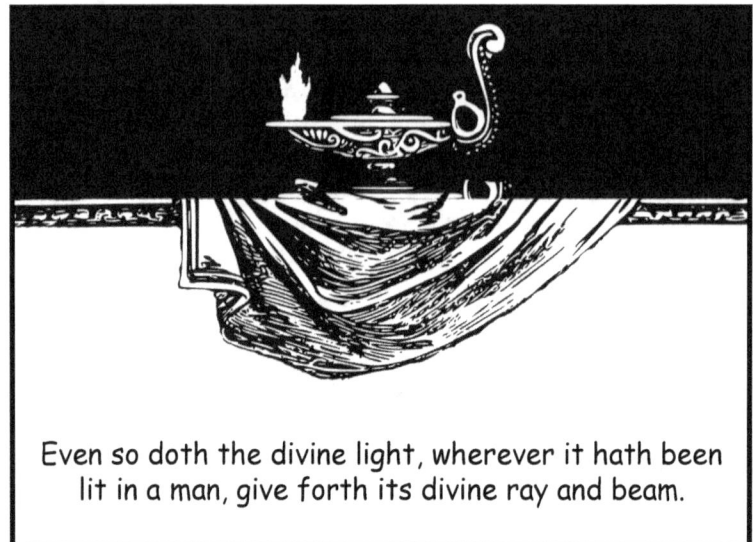

Even so doth the divine light, wherever it hath been lit in a man, give forth its divine ray and beam.

with its nature, to give light thereby to men, even so doth the divine light, wherever it hath been lit in a man, give forth its divine ray and beam. The nature of this light, however, is true, divine righteousness, brightness and truth, which is shed abroad by the lantern which is the Church of Christ, more brightly and clearly than by the sun, to give light to all men.[73]

I would like to repeat my prayer from chapter 2:

Father in heaven, I am nothing. But if you can use a donkey to speak to a wayward prophet, then perhaps you can use me, weak as I am, to help bring revival. In Jesus' name, please use this book to touch and change the Christians in America. I pray that everyone will read with an open heart – especially the church leaders. Amen.

---

73   Peter Riedemann, *Confession of Faith*, 1970, Plough Publishing House, pp. 39-40.

Come Holy Spirit

The Holy Spirit came at Pentecost
He came in mighty fullness then
His witness through believers won the lost
And multitudes were born again
The early Christians scattered over the world
They preached the Gospel fearlessly
Though some were martyred and to lions hurled
They marched along in victory

Come Holy Spirit
Dark is the hour
We need your filling
Your love and your mighty power
Move now among us
Stir us we pray
Come Holy Spirit
Revive the Church today.[74]

---

[74] By John W. Peterson. Lyrics © 1971 John W. Peterson Music Company. All rights reserved. Used by permission.

Chapter 16

Challenge to the Nominal Christian

Follow me, the Saviour calleth;
Come to me, I am the way!
What is lacking I will give you;
Trust in me and watch and pray!
Follow me in true submission;
I have borne all your transgression;
Learn of me, both great and small,
Meekly, humbly hear my call.

Thru this life I've gone before you,
Serving not earth's vanity;
So should all now choose my virtue
And my true disciples be.
Follow me with cheerful spirit
That my kingdom ye inherit.
Yea, forsake the highway broad;
Follow me on heaven's road.

Why is there this anxious striving
For the treasures of this earth?
By God's word they all will perish,
Honor, pleasure, wealth and mirth.
And I, who have life eternal,
Joy and blessedness supernal,
Find so few who will obey
On the straight and narrow way!

I call weeping: "Tribes and nations,
O that all could understand
And would come to seek salvation,
Would obey my kind command!"
For the day is drawing nearer
When the disobeying hearers
Who the truth have not believed,
In false hope they were deceived.

When the words by prophets spoken,
Their fulfillment then shall find:
"Lo! Their vision I have broken
And confused their heart and mind!"
Woe to ev'ry willful being
Who is constantly pursuing
A perverse and sinful way,
And in selfish pride does stay.

Therefore, all ye human beings,
Hear today the Saviour's word;
He came for the poor lost sinner
Who with joy His message heard.
Come, believe! Be meek and lowly,
For His Word is true and holy;
Who believes Him is made free
Here and in eternity.

Sing, all ye who are persuaded
By the power of His call!
O, be glad; for you are aided
By His hand through dangers all.
Not a sparrow ever falleth
Lest it be that God alloweth;
So rejoice exceedingly
For His kingdom yours shall be.

Walk thus, cheering one another,
Little flock, e'en to the end;
If ye see a stumbling brother,
Helpful word and hand extend;
Filled with God's own mighty fullness,
Follow Christ in holy stillness;
Sing to Him a "Gloria!"
And rejoice, "Hallelujah!"[75]

—*Zion's Harp* #95

---

[75] Used by the permission of Apostolic Christian Publications.

Oh, magnify the
LORD
with me,
And let us exalt
His name
together.

~Psalm 34:3

Illustration Credits

Page 4 - Public domain photograph.

Page 8 - Public domain illustration.

Page 16 - Public domain illustration by Gustave Doré.

Page 18 - Public domain illustration by Jan Luyken (from *Martyrs Mirror*).

Page 25 - Photograph by Erik Wesner; used by permission.

Page 27 - Photograph copyright © Andrew V. Ste. Marie.

Page 36 - From *Foxe's Book of Martyrs*; public domain.

Page 37 - Public domain.

Page 43 - Public domain.

Page 54 - Photograph copyright © Andrew V. Ste. Marie.

Page 61 - Public domain illustration by Gustave Doré.

Page 70 - Public domain clipart.

Page 77 - Public domain illustration by Mike Atnip.

Page 91 - Public domain portrait by Lucas Cranach dem Älteren in 1529.

Page 93 - Public domain.

Page 94 - Public domain.

Page 95 - Public domain painting by C. C. A. Christensen.

Page 101 - Photograph by morguefile.com user taylorschlades.

Page 113 - Public domain clipart.

Page 115 - Public domain illustration by J. William Turner.

Page 122 - Public domain photos.

Page 130 - Public domain illustration by Mike Atnip.

Page 136 - Public domain illustration by Mike Atnip.

Page 142 - Public domain clip art.

Cover by Mike Atnip.

*For more excellent titles,
call or write for a free catalog:*

Sermon on the Mount Publishing
P.O. Box 246
Manchester, MI 48158
(734) 428-0488

the-witness@sbcglobal.net

www.kingdomreading.com

www.ingramcontent.com/pod-product-compliance
Lightning Source LLC
Chambersburg PA
CBHW052035070526
44584CB00016B/2055